THE DREAD INFERNO

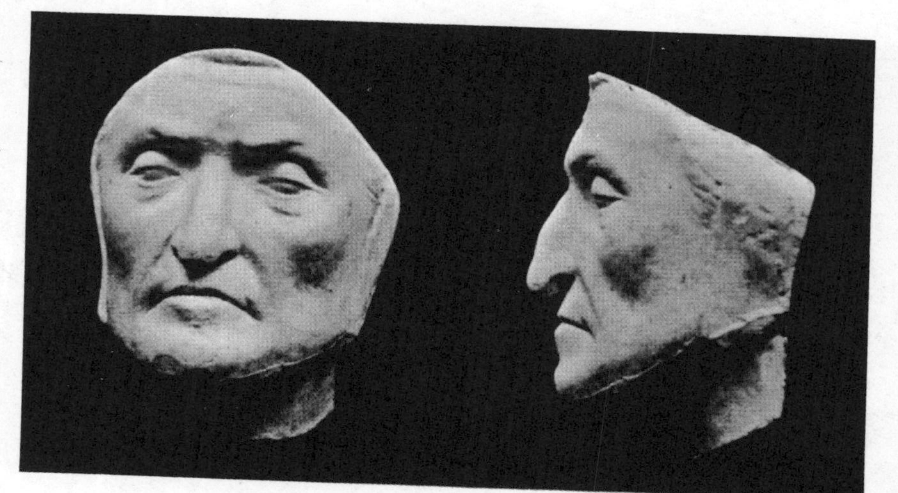

CAST OF DANTE'S FACE TAKEN AFTER DEATH

(*From a photograph by Ed. Alinari*)

THE DREAD INFERNO

NOTES FOR BEGINNERS
IN THE STUDY OF DANTE

BY

M. ALICE WYLD

"BENE ASCOLTA CHI LA NOTA"

WITH FRONTISPIECE

KENNIKAT PRESS
Port Washington, N. Y./London

THE DREAD INFERNO

First published in 1904
Reissued in 1969 by Kennikat Press
Library of Congress Catalog Card No: 73-101032
SBN 8046-0699-4

Manufactured by Taylor Publishing Company   Dallas, Texas

PREFACE

THE following Notes have a humble and definite aim. They are intended solely for the use of Beginners in the study of Dante.

For some years I have read Dante's *Comedy* with Classes, composed chiefly of those who know little of Dante. Not infrequently I have at the outset been met by such objections as: " How can you commend Dante as a spiritual teacher? The *Inferno* is nothing better than a picture of hideous physical torments." Or again : " I cannot see how a man who delights in putting his enemies into Hell can see truly the meaning of Life."

After studying the *Inferno* carefully some of these objectors have come to see that Dante " puts " no one in Hell, but sorrowfully shows us how men—some of them beloved and honoured friends or heroes—put themselves there. They have seen, too, how the picture of ugly physical misery is given only as the symbol of a miserable spiritual condition from which Dante would fain save us. They have seen the whole, in fact, in a new light, as a vision of the results in the soul of man of an evil choice, results which are real now on earth, but hidden from us by many coverings of circumstance.

To help to bring these and other truths to the surface, and to lead a few of my pupils to read on and to delight in what Dante delighted in, the Vision of the Ideal of Human Life, as he tells it in the *Paradiso*, has been a great pleasure. I now print these Notes on the *Inferno* in the hope that a few readers may do the same. In Dante's words they will, I believe, find one of the deepest and purest sources of that Water of Life which wells up for us through the hearts and minds of our great teachers.

I have taken my quotations from the three parts of the *Comedy* from the prose translations of Dr. Carlyle (amended), Mr. Thos. Okey, and Mr. P. H. Wicksteed, and I thank Messrs. J. M. Dent and Co. for their courteous permission to do so. To Mr. Paget Toynbee's *Dante Dictionary* I am indebted for much useful information.

To Mr. P. H. Wicksteed I owe a further debt.
Many years ago I read his beautiful little book,
Six Sermons on Dante ; it sent me back to the
poet with fresh eyes and hopes.   More helpful
still I have found what I call his Counsel of
Perfection, given, I believe, to all his classes.
It is : " Read Dante's own words first and last,
and the words of Dante's teachers, rather than
those of his commentators." This Counsel I now
pass on to others.   If any who read these
words will close this book and give themselves
to the following of this Counsel they will have
a rich reward for their labours, a reward which
will remain with them in the day when they
" shall call *this* time ancient."

CONTENTS

INTRODUCTION

O abbondante grazia, ond' io presunsi
Ficcar lo viso per la luce eterna
Tanto che la veduta vi consunsi !
Nel suo profondo vidi che s'interna,
Legato con amore in un volume,
Ciò che per l'universo si squaderna.

Par., xxxiii. 82–87.

IN this passage, one of the most sympathetic of English Dante scholars[1] finds the proper title for Dante's works, "An Encyclopædia bound into one volume by Love." It is this harmony and mutual dependence of the great poet's writings that makes Dante his own best commentator. Each of his works, great or small, sheds light on the rest, and perhaps no one of them can be completely understood without a knowledge of some at least of the others. This is specially true of the *Vita Nuova*, the *Convivio*, and the *Divine Comedy;*

[1] P. H. Wicksteed.

these are members one of another in many ways, though we also recognise in each of them a very distinct individual life.

It is, of course, possible to enjoy intensely the *Comedy* without any knowledge of the minor works, or to love the *Vita Nuova* without having read the *Comedy*. Most of us, however, in studying Dante, have recourse to some commentator or lecturer to aid our first steps. If we find this necessary, I think we shall find also that a repeated study of what Dante has himself written will more fully equip us for a joyous and invigorating understanding of, say, the mystic imagery of the *Paradiso*, than do the words of any commentator, read without such direct contact with the various developments of the poet's own thoughts. This study is no labour of Hercules, as all Dante's writings can be contained within the limits of a closely packed octavo volume.

The more we read, on certain lines, the more our pleasure will be increased. We ought to gain some knowledge of the history of the time, at least in Italy, and if the first cantos of the *Inferno*, or some chapter of the

Convivio, send us off on a search into one of the treatises of Aristotle, "the Master of those who know"—his *Ethics* perhaps, or his *Politics*—we shall have a great reward in lofty and enlightening thoughts that permanently enrich and uplift the mind, and that shed much light on the method and outlook of our poet.

We find the leading ideas of Dante's minor works re-embodied and often more fully developed in the *Comedy*. This is not to say that these minor works may not have a certain completeness in themselves. The *Vita Nuova* is a gem, perfect in its cutting and setting, yet it is also a promise of something greater to come. The treatise *De Monarchia* is also, in a sense, finished and complete, but we find its finest thoughts again in the *Comedy*, idealised and carried out in their most spiritual application. On the other hand, the treatise *De Vulgare Eloquio* and the *Convivio* are only fragments, and remain such, probably because the *Comedy* was taking shape in Dante's thought and poetic imagination, and was at once absorbing all that could have completed these earlier writings and transcending them in substance and in scope.

Certainly the *Convivio* seems to be abandoned partly because Dante had gained a deeper thought about the moral life, and because a more vital and poetic view of the Universe had developed itself before him as his soul was exercised by strenuous living, and his imagination grew more vivid and mature. One point may illustrate this. Dante tells us in the *Convivio* that he writes, in part, to clear himself from blame for sins of the flesh of which he was accused. With this we compare the self-knowledge shown at the meeting with Forese on the Mount of Cleansing, and the deep and piercing repentance in the scene with Beatrice in the Earthly Paradise, and we are at once conscious of a deeper insight and a nobler standpoint.

Purg., xxiii. 115-120.

Purg., xxxi. 16-21, 31-36, 85-90.

What is the unifying element in all Dante's work? Surely it is the aim which inspires him throughout. This aim is twofold. In the first place, Dante seeks to express in beautiful form and language the grand conception he has formed of the Harmony of the Universe. In his Art he is the "Grandchild of the Deity," and his task is to give us a living presentation

C. xi. 105.

of the Divine Idea of the Universe. This idea is of a perfect harmony. The Universe is harmonious in the law of its being, that is the law of a constant mutual giving and receiving of the divine power; it is harmonious in the perfect balance of Knowledge and Love, in the fulfilment of judgment and mercy in a perfect Justice. In the second place, he seeks in every possible way to forward the practical fulfilment of the Divine Idea on earth and in the lives of men.

The first aim realises itself finally in the glorious vision of the *Paradiso*. This is the perfect fruit of Dante's divinely inspired poetic imagination. The form and mode of expression of the vision belong to the age in which Dante lived, but Dante so transcended, in imagination and in mental attitude, all others of that age, while he most perfectly assimilated the thoughts and imagery with which it supplied him, that the lovely and passionate cantos of the *Paradiso* have become the most perfect spiritual poem for every age that believes in God and in the Human soul.

The second aim was very consciously present

in Dante's mind in most of his writings. In the treatise *De Vulgare Eloquio* he is full of the desire to harmonise and ennoble the dialects of Italy, and fuse them into a common tongue, that so the unification of men may be advanced. In the *De Monarchia* the effort is farther reaching : it is to bring men to recognise in theory and to realise in practice the harmony essential to a true political life. To Dante, as to Aristotle, ethics are the introduction to politics. Man is not completely man till he is a good citizen, and this citizenship demands recognition of himself and of other men as units of a great whole, composed of many parts, and gathered under one head, the ideal Emperor, who, just and disinterested, makes peace and justice to flourish on the earth. In the *Comedy* we have the call to men to see, admire, and seek after the perfect harmony of all life, moral and intellectual, individual and social, in the love which flows from the vision of the Divine Reality, and fulfils itself in mutual service and in perfect oneness with the Will of God.

V.E., ii.
2, 83 ; 93 94

Again, in the treatise *De Vulgare Eloquio* Dante tells us that he chose righteousness as the theme of his poetry. To Can Grande, his *Ep.*, x. 11. friend and helper, to whom he dedicates the *Paradiso*, he tells the meaning of the *Comedy*. Taken literally, it is the story of individual souls; in its far more important meaning—the moral and spiritually allegorical meaning—it is the picture of Man "as by freewill meriting and demeriting, he is subject to justice rewarding and punishing." His object in presenting this § 16. picture is to remove those who live in the world from a state of misery to a state of gladness; it is, he affirms, a most practical poem, dwelling in the purely ethical regions.

In this life we do not see clearly the retributive effects of actions ; in Dante's vision we see the crop that really springs from each kind of seed. In the supposed state of certain souls after death he finds the symbol of the true state of all such souls always. A great modern realist has told us that the only sermon that can impress is the story of what is. Dante, a greater realist, because he paints the most perfect loveliness as well as the basest ugliness, and sees the beauty to be deeper and greater than the ugliness, practically says the same. He finds that to see the great realities of Hell, and Purgatory, and Paradise, with an understanding heart, is to penetrate to the meaning of human life. Such an experience will deliver a man from the darksome wood of moral, social, intellectual, and spiritual error in which licentiousness, pride, and greed have entangled him.

Especially perhaps, in reading the *Inferno* we need to keep in view the range of Dante's aim : we need to recognise it as only one note in the perfect chord of the *Comedy*. Many people know Dante only from the *Inferno*, and yet, without the light shed on it by the thought of the *Purgatorio* and the *Paradiso*, without the recognition that Dante's conception of the Universe is of a Harmony, not of a Discord, that his final utterance is of Hope and Love, not of Hate and Despair, the *Inferno* cannot be rightly understood.

We must try to realise what it is that Dante wishes to give us in this, the prologue to his great poem. It has been said that in Dante's Hell, owing to the nature of the framework, we lose a sense of infinity; but perhaps there is apt to be an unhelpful vagueness in our minds

when we speak of infinity; what Dante gives C. xxxiii. 129–132.
us is a sense of the reality of the eternal things.
When he makes us see that a man, seemingly
alive in Florence, or shall we say in London,
may really have his soul in Hell if it is given
up to hellish feelings, he makes the most superficial of us pause and think. To Dante himself
it is all more real than to the least superficial
of us. He weeps, and quails, and faints, as he
realises the fruit of sin. So deeply did he bear
the impress of his work that people looking at
him said he had been in Hell.

The *Inferno* then, represents the eternal,
that is, the real or spiritual rather than the
phenomenal or circumstantial results of evil
choices and acts. Retribution is its keynote, as
Hope is that of the *Purgatorio*, and joyous Love
of the *Paradiso*. But as the hopeful suffering
of the *Purgatorio* is touched by joy and love,
so even the gloomy walls of the *Inferno* are lit
by gleams of beauty and of hope, and, in one
sense, it too is a Song of Deliverance: the
deliverance of Dante's soul through his experiences in that gloomy pilgrimage, the deliverance
of every human soul that shares with Dante in

a cleansing vision of the horror and dead isolation of the self-centred life.

The subject of the poem is in no way peculiar to Dante. In all ages men have been fascinated by the problem of the soul's life beyond the grave. In all ages men have seen visions and dreamed dreams, and before Dante's day Christian or Ecclesiastical teaching had gradually shaped these visions into a more and more definite form. The unseen world had grown into Hell, Purgatory, and Paradise, sometimes further subdivisions had been craved to satisfy the ethical sense of the dreamer.[1] How many of such visions were known to Dante is not important. The *Æneid* of Virgil was in some ways an inspiration, and he evidently refers to the *Apocalypse of St. Paul;* many other visions have points of resemblance to his *Inferno.*

It is not his subject, not the scenery of his poem, that raises Dante so far above all these other dreamers. It is the moral and spiritual content of his dream. The Vision of the

---

[1] For an interesting account of many of these visions from Babylonian times see *Forerunners of Dante*, by Marcus Dods, M. A.

Paradiso, which is that for which all the rest exists, is no mere list of virtues and of their more or less appropriate rewards. It is a vision of that which is Eternal Life, the Reality that exists behind and within all the passing phenomena and gives them value. It is the flower of purest poetry for that Age as for many Ages to come. It sums up the best aspirations and deepest thoughts of the Middle Ages on political, moral, and spiritual questions. Yet it is not only mediæval; it is almost certainly a spiritual power in hundreds of lives in the twentieth century for one it inspired in the fourteenth. It breathes such a keen spiritual life that it imparts vitalising force. As we read the Empyrean Vision earth's limitations and discords and separations fade For the moment we see the divine reality of Life and are satisfied.

The framework of the *Inferno* is Dante's own. The earth to him, as to all of that age, is the unmoving centre of the Universe, and round it the heavens revolve, bearing their planets and fixed stars. In Dante's scheme the Eastern Hemisphere is land, having Jerusalem as its centre.

Hell is entered somewhere near Jerusalem; it is in the form of an inverted cone, and its apex is exactly beneath the Island of Purgatory, which *Inf.*, C. rises in the Western Hemisphere of water. At xxxiv. the end of the *Inferno* Dante tells us how Lucifer fell on the Western Hemisphere, and how, in fear and shame, the land fled away, veiling itself under the waters; it rose on our Eastern Hemisphere, leaving in the Western Sea only an island, which was to become the Mount of Purgatory. On its summit this island bore the Earthly Paradise where Man was, in his turn, to undergo, and fail under, temptation. Yet this Earthly Paradise remained, and the story of Man's restoration to its life of freedom and his ascent to the more perfect life of completed Knowledge and Love is the story of Dante's *Comedy*.

THE DARKSOME WOOD AND THE HEAVENLY HELPERS

Nel mezzo del cammin di nostra vita
Mi ritrovai per una selva oscura,
Chè la diritta via era smarrita.

Inferno, C. i. 1–3.

Io son Beatrice che ti faccio andare ;
Vegno di loco, ove tornar disio ;
Amor mi mosse, che mi fa parlare.

Inferno, C. ii. 70–72.

IN the first line of the *Inferno* we are given Canto i.
the ideal date of the poem as 1300. We
know this because, in another place, Dante fixes
thirty-five as the central year of man's natural
life, and Dante was born in 1265. The season is
the vernal equinox, the perfect season, when life
is at its fullest; the season chosen by God for
the Creation of the world, and for the fulfilment
in time of the Redemption of man. Of course
this is not the real date of the whole poem
which made Dante "lean through many a

Par., xxv.
1–3.

year," and he himself deals very freely with it, writing sometimes, as in this opening passage, as at the ideal date, at others, as when he came

C. xix. 79–84.

among the Simonists, as at the actual time of writing, which must have been after the death of Clement V. in 1314; sometimes in the same way in the *Purgatorio* and *Paradiso*, where the date is still later.

In the mid-time then of his life, Dante came to himself in a dark and dreary wood, where

Conv., iv.
24 119.127.

the straight way was lost. Like the Adolescent, newly entering the misleading wood of this life, he is in need of guidance; indeed, he is in sorer need than such an one, for he once knew the way, and has not only lost it, but seeks it again with eyes darkened and powers weakened by his own fault. This rough and stubborn wood may, in one sense, symbolise the evil condition of the world resulting from bad government and unchecked greed; but, without doubt, it also

Cf. *Purg.*,
xxiii. 115–
123; xxx.
124–141.

signifies that lost condition into which Dante had come by the easy but crooked path of self-indulgence and worldly pursuits after the death of Beatrice. Having come to himself in a night of great confusion of soul, in the morning

Dante has a vision of beauty; he sees a delect-able mountain, the eyes of his soul perceive the *v. 77.* truly happy life of earthly righteousness; God's Sun is shining on the mountain-top, it is the Earthly Paradise.

In the first place, Dante tells us here of the state of his own soul, but through our sympathy with him, he would lead us to think of Man as a sinful soul; and the story of his personal experience is also the story of how Man can be turned from sin to righteousness. The sym-bolism is quite simple. The Sun is ever to Dante the true symbol of God, for " Nothing *Conv., iii. 12 52 53.* sensible in all the world is more worthy to become the symbol of God than the Sun, which with sensible light enlightens itself and all bodies celestial and elemental as God with light intellectual enlightens first Himself and all celestial and other intelligences."

Dante tries of his own effort to mount the hill, but as he climbs painfully upward he meets three dangerous and evil beasts, the *vv. 31–53.* panther, the lion, and the wolf. These crea-tures are a favourite mediæval symbol of evil; they are, of course, first Jeremiah's avenging *Jer. v. 6.*

creatures, and they have been used with varying application. St. Jerome gives them a historical as well as a moral meaning, applying them to the Babylonian, the Medo - Persian, and the Greek Powers, as Dante is supposed to have applied them to Florence, France, and the Papal Power. The deeper and more constant meaning in the *Comedy* is the moral one. The panther, less frightful at first with its gay and spotted hair, is probably lust, the fleshly sins of youth ; this is the more likely because Dante tells us, at a later stage of the journey, that he had tried to conquer it with the cord of St.

vv. 37-43. Francis. In the glad morning sunshine of the springtime, remembering how the glad Creator first at this season made all things fair and good, Dante hopes to conquer this evil creature, but the lion of Pride, a great enemy to Dante person-ally, now comes to bar his way ; and worst,

vv. 49-51. most cruel and deadly, the wolf "full of all cravings in her leanness." There may be a

Cf. C. vi. 74; question as to the nature of the panther, which
xv. 68. sometimes seems to signify envy, but there is none as to the evil nature of the wolf, the deadly

v. 51. Avarice which has made many live in sorrow.

We meet her again in the circle cursed because C. vii. 8.
of ill-spent money, and in Purgatory, among *Purg.*, xx. 10-15.
the Avaricious and Prodigal, Dante cries out
" Accurst be thou, she-wolf of old, that hast
more prey than all the other beasts, for thy
hunger endlessly deep! O heaven, in whose
revolution it seems that conditions here below
are thought to be changed, when will he come
through whom she shall depart?"

Dante now despairs of attaining a happy
earthly life. Here, as all through his vision
of evil and of good, he feels that cupidity is the
chief cause of loss of spiritual life; that is to
say, the greedy pursuit of material things so
absorbs and darkens the soul, that love and
aspiration and freedom die, and hate and ambition and servitude of the spirit dwell in their
place.

And now, when driven down to the darkness
of self-despair, the dismayed poet meets with
Virgil. He is at once a beloved master and
a great symbolic figure, and we must pause
to consider what such a meeting means to
Dante. Dante's view of the rights and duties
of the Church and the Empire are known to us

c

from the *Convivio*, the treatise *De Monarchia*, and many passages in the *Comedy*. It is a very lofty view. The Church is Christ's vicegerent on earth to lead man to the perfect blessedness of the spiritual life, the life of contemplation, the vision of God. The Emperor receives his power as directly from God as does the Pope, and his office, which no man can take from him, and which he may not lay down himself, is to rule in justice so that peace on earth may be possible, so that men may live perfectly the life of citizenship, the active life of moral rectitude.

As things were, Dante saw very clearly and sadly that neither of these great ends was accomplished. The Church was full of avarice, mother of simony; full of self-indulgent vice; careless for the spiritual good of her children, and greedy for temporal power and self-aggrandisement. The Emperor had let slip his responsibilities, and, instead of fulfilling his rôle as the one quite disinterested ruler who had all men's welfare in his thoughts, he did not even visit Italy, the fairest portion of his heritage, and was absorbed in narrow personal aims, while faction and turmoil reigned in the place of justice and peace. This being so, Dante sought to lead the minds of men back to the great thoughts and principles that under-lie and inspire the idea of Church and Empire. The deep foundation of the Church is that Divine Philosophy or Theology which can lead us to the vision of God. Of this no creature but Beatrice can be the final representative. Beatrice, who, while on earth, had led Dante's youthful life towards all that was of the Spirit and the Truth.

The Empire is founded on that noble Human Philosophy which, true also and worthy, leads us up to that true moral life which has its abode in the Earthly Paradise. This Human Philosophy Dante found in the teaching of Aristotle, Virgil, Boethius, a teaching incom-plete but trustworthy, leading to the Divine Philosophy, and falling out of sight only when absorbed and fulfilled in that higher lore. This Human Philosophy is here represented by Virgil. The great Latin poet, and not the great Greek philosopher, is our guide through the *Inferno*, though everywhere Aristotle is recognised as the great teacher. The reasons for this are not far to seek. Virgil was a great personality in the Middle Ages, his teaching was considered almost Christian, and he was regarded as really foretelling the Advent of Christ. To Dante he was a living and beloved person, a great teacher in their common art, the imaginative historian of that Roman Empire which was Dante's ideal of all that was strong, wise, and God-given in government ; above all, he had played a great part in his personal life. When Dante, downcast and bewildered after Beatrice's death, was in sore danger of moral and intellectual shipwreck, Virgil had led him to the study of Aristotle, had given him a true insight into the inner meaning of History, and a true view of Human Life. Of this we have more than a hint in the *Convivio*, and, as we follow his guidance through Hell and Purgatory, there is spread out before us, as in a panoramic view, all that Virgil did for Dante. At last, his work done, he vanishes, and his pupil, *Purg.*,xxvii. crowned and mitred, master of his own moral 139–142. and spiritual life, enters into communion with his Heavenly Lady, the glorified Beatrice of the Paradisaic vision.

It is this wise and gentle teacher whom Dante meets in the moment of dismay; he is very evidently no mere symbol but also a true man. Here, as later, he is the poet, the glory and light of other poets, noble in word and in deed, praised by men and praiseworthy at the throne of God; courteous and wise, gentle and unselfish, his character lives and glows for us in these pages. Now he tells Dante that he cannot go straight up the delectable mountain but must travel by a harder road of deep experience. He must learn the horror of evil in its results in human souls; learn too, the beauty of holiness in the willing suffering of those who aspire; and, finally, led by one worthier than he, learn to rejoice in the vision of the perfect life of Love, the glad dance and song of man's true life in God.

Virgil's first word of cheer to Dante is his *vv.* 100-105. prophecy of the coming of a Hound that shall chase away the wolf of avarice from the land. It has just been explained that Virgil does not represent the imperial authority, but rather the principles that underlie and support that authority; neither does he seem to be the practical reformer, though his teaching may inspire such an one. Now, the coming of the Hound is prophesied in the tone which Dante uses when he hopes for a definite and speedy deliverance, when he feels that Providence will soon bring succour to the faction-tormented, vice-plagued land. This succour Dante certainly desired and hoped for in the person of an ideal ruler, a true Emperor, and probably this may be the Hound of Virgil's prophecy. Perhaps, on the other hand, he may refer to the great Ghibelline leader, Can Grande. Can Grande had gained some success in arms in 1314, when *Par.*, xvii. Dante was probably perfecting the *Inferno*, 76-90. and, notable in his acts, " careless of money and of toils and munificent in his deeds," he filled Dante with hope, and answers well to the description of the implacable hunter of avarice. We may not be mistaken in either interpretation or in both; through and beyond both may gleam the thought of certain deliverance from evil, because a greater than patriot chief or ideal Emperor, even Christ Himself, " is work-

ing in the abyss," and will reign till all enemies
are put under His feet.

Meantime, turning back from the hill, Dante
and Virgil pace on through the wood, and
Virgil wakens hope in Dante's heart by other
words of cheer, a sober hope of deliverance
through many difficulties.   Incidentally he
touches on his own condition ; but, in describ-
ing his own limitation, the chief point dwelt *vv.* 118-129.
on is at once the omnipresence of God and
His special presence, in a spiritual sense, where
all hearts own His sway.   This thought links
us at once with the thought of the *Purgatorio*
and the *Paradiso.* God is "not circumscribed
but through His greater love for His first works
on high."   The material of the Universe takes *Purg.,* xi.
more or less of the impress of the Divine *Par.,* i. 1-3;
Image as it is pure and good or full of alloy. ii. 127-132.
God can be most where souls can most receive
of His Essence.   In all the Universe He rules
indeed, but His Will is only done in the ideal
sense where the desires and wills of men and *Par.,* xxxiii.
angels are rolled, as a wheel that moveth equally, 142-148.
by the Love that moves the sun and the other
planets.

vv. 130-135. The first canto of the *Inferno* ends with a personal note. Dante is set on deliverance, he will boldly face all to gain admission at the gate of entrance to the Mountain of Purification. This is his aim through all his journeying; he tells it here to Virgil, and he tells it again to Casella, whom he meets on the strand of the blessed Isle: "To return here once again where I am, make I this journey."

Purg., ii. 91, 92.

Canto ii. The second canto opens with the closing day; the dusky air darkens round Dante and Virgil as they turn their steps towards the realm of sorrow; the sun sets on earth as they near the world of spiritual darkness. When they shall emerge into the land of hopeful aspiration, the sun will be rising in glad promise of life-giving light; and when Dante mounts to the Paradisaic gladness it will be at the noontide hour, the perfect hour when the pulse of life beats fullest.

vv. 4, 6. We cannot but notice that Dante does not here distrust the powers of mind and memory as he does in the *Purgatorio,* and more and more in the *Paradiso.* He dreads the enterprise, he doubts his power of soul to bear the encounter with evil, but he does not feel the intellectual inadequacy of his understanding so fully expressed in the *Paradiso*, nor the difficulty of carrying away the vision in memory, and of telling it in words.

In the opening of the *Paradiso* Dante tells us: "I have seen things which whoso descendeth from up there hath not knowledge nor power to retell; because, as it draweth nigh to its desire, our intellect sinketh so deep, that memory cannot go back upon the track." *Par.*, i. 4-9.

Again, when he meets Cacciaguida, he tells how "Then—joyous both to hearing and to sight—the spirit added things to his beginning I understood not, so profound his speech; neither of choice hid he himself from me, but of necessity, for above the target of mortals his thought took its place." *Par.*, xv. 37-42.

Among the contemplatives Dante is told of certain truths, that not only can he not fathom them, "But that soul in heaven which is most illuminated, that Seraph who hath his eye most fixed on God, will not give satisfaction to thy question; because so far within the abyss of the eternal statute lieth the thing thou askest that *Par.*, xxi. 91-96.

from all created vision it is cut off." When he has looked on Christ, and so is made mighty to bear the brightness of Beatrice's smile, he says: "I was as one who cometh to himself *Par.*, xxiii. 49-51; 61-63. from a forgotten vision, and doth strive in vain to bring it back unto his mind. . . . And, therefore, figuring Paradise, needs must the sacred poem make a leap, as who should find his pathway intercepted." Many other passages tell of the same sense of insufficiency, and at last, when the final vision bursts on Dante's sight and he would fain tell us of its gladdening and soul-satisfying beauty, he feels "Now shall my *Par.*, xxxiii. 106-108. speech fall farther short even of what I can emember than an infant's who still bathes his tongue at breast." The best things are the greatest and the deepest. Evil is terrible, but it is more superficial than Good; Good is unfathomable. The whole Universe means harmony and joy; it is the expression of God's love bursting out into manifold forms that enjoy and respond to that love. Evil is a measurable thing; the circles of Hell may be told in miles or yards, the Paradise of God transcends all limits of time or space. The groans of the sinful rend the heart, but they are easily understood, and at their loudest can be compared with ordinary earthly sounds, whereas, in Saturn, the song of the blessed contemplatives must be hushed lest Dante should be deafened by its sonorous rapture, and the smile of Beatrice must be withheld lest Dante's *Par.*, xxi. mortal sight be darkened for ever by its blaze. 61–63.

On the first realisation of his own evil case and of the deliverance to be won, Dante was full of eagerness to set forth on his journey, but soon discouragement succeeds to zeal. Others have undertaken this journey, but that *vv.* 10–42. does not comfort him. Æneas was worthy to be upheld in all his great experiences, for he was ancestor of the founder of Rome, and was strengthened to learn things that were to establish the Empire and the Papacy. This passage is one of those which shows that Dante felt that Empire and Papacy alike got their authority direct from God, and were most intimately connected with one another in their functions, but its interest for us is that it throws light on Dante's view of his own place in the world. He feels himself called to a great mission, which

has both a political and a religious side.   In his
Epistle to the Italian Cardinals, Dante, like
Jeremiah, and in his very words, laments the
evils wrought by cupidity in the Church, he
speaks of the divine mission of the Church as
neglected, and of himself, "the least of the
sheep, but at least not rich," as full of zeal for
God's house, and moved by God's grace to
exhort the priests of God to a like zeal.   As
the man born blind confessed Christ while the
Pharisees persecuted both, so he must speak
out to those to whom the hungry sheep look
up and are not fed.   The Cardinals have left
Gregory and Augustine, Dionysius and Bede,
because such teachers were a rebuke to their
lives.   Dante, the mouthpiece of many who
share his feelings, hopes that shame may yet
wake in their souls, the *Verecundia* of the
Convivio, that shame which begets penitence,
a penitence so bitter it hinders from the like
fault in the future.   He hopes, and so he makes
a passionate appeal to them to rise to a true
love of the Spiritual Church and a true love
of the fatherland.   In the Epistle to Can
Grande, too, Dante speaks of his mission, and

his message, and of his confidence that God, who makes His sun to shine on the evil and the good, will show His glory to him, though he is a sinful man, and will give him true words to speak. Dante feels he is called of God, and it is with God's great elect souls that he compares himself. Æneas and Paul visited the unseen world, but who am I? "I am not Æneas. I am not Paul; neither myself nor others deem me worthy."

We think of Dante as essentially a strong man, one who stood four-square against the changes and chances of life, but here he describes himself as conscious of a great timidity, fearful and diffident, in two minds about his task, and shrinking under the criticism of others. Again and again he shows that he knew himself to be over-sensitive to the opinion of others. Later on in their journey Virgil urges him *Purg.*, v. 10–15. sharply to follow on, and let the people talk, to stand "as a firm tower which never shakes its summit for blast of winds," and Dante owns himself in fault by the blush of an honest shame. In the *Convivio* he tells us how, cast *Conv.*, i. 3 1-48. out from the most sweet breast of Florence, the most beautiful and famous daughter of Rome, he was poor and dependent, flouted and despised till his sensitive spirit grew sore and tender, and he cared too much what men said and thought.   Here, like his prototype Jeremiah, when the Word of the Lord comes, and he knows he must say rough things to the great and powerful, Dante feels "I cannot speak, for I am a child."

This state of mind is rebuked by Virgil, the great-souled, as pusillanimity. It is not humility. Dante is called on to act, not to question. If a mission is committed to him that is the one important thing ; he must fulfil it as he can, not as he would. With the rebuke comes also the encouragement. The mission is indeed a high one, but it is from on high and will not be fulfilled by Dante in his own unaided strength. *vv.* 49 *sqq.* Virgil now tells the story of his coming to the wandering, bewildered poet. His story brings out one of the most beautiful of Dante's thoughts about the spiritual world. In the Spiritual Universe there are no impenetrable barriers. All Life is one. This is one of Dante's great teachings, and we must not miss its force. The accident of death does not sever soul from soul: in some way, a mystery but a great reality, we help and hinder one another still, we love and claim and meet one another in the spiritual life. Heaven and Hell are parts of one great whole, and when all is fulfilled it will be shown as a harmonious whole. Dante did not understand this when Beatrice died, and so he tried to satisfy his soul-hunger with the husks of worldly affairs, and self-indulgence on the lower levels. In Paradise he will fully attain, and know that time and space are powerless over kindred souls. In God, all souls that aspire are near, because they are akin one to the other, though circumstances may seem to separate them as far as is the region that thundereth most high from the lowest deep of the sea.

Here already this truth is dawning. Beatrice, seated at the feet of the Blessed Virgin in Paradise, loves her friend in the dark, tangled wood of a sin-snared life: "My friend, but not of fortune." She is in touch, too, with Virgil, the noble though not Christian teacher. She can descend into Hell and rise again to her seat on high. Nor is Virgil cut off from the Communion of Saints; he is used for noble service by the God he knew so imperfectly. Beatrice will often praise him for his work before the Lord she loves. Man's whole nature, too, is one; there is no divorce between Reason and Faith. Reason, Morality, and the spiritual life of Faith are all united. The individual soul too, draws to itself all spiritual forces and unifies the worlds. The soul, grown conscious of its need, lays claim upon the heavenly spirits to help it to the joy it is made for, and that claim is recognised. "I am Beatrice, and it is love that moves me to speak." Beatrice and Love; these give its meaning to the *Comedy*, without them we had had no *Comedy*; the tragedy of exile, the passion of patriotism we should have seen, and surely some fruit of intellect and genius, but not this *Comedy* that is so divine.

But who and what is Beatrice? Some say she is a mere creature of Dante's brain, she is just a symbol of Theology or Divine Philosophy, she has nothing to do with any real Beatrice Portinari, and we only confuse our minds by admitting such an idea. If we get rid of the maiden Beatrice and retain only a phantom symbol of Wisdom, the history of Dante's mind can be all consistently mapped out; the changes of his opinions from orthodoxy to a supposed scepticism and back again to orthodoxy can be fitted into a plan, and the *Vita Nuova*, the *Convivio*, and the *Comedy* form the three great stages of Dante's intellectual and religious development. Perhaps this may be so, though this view only gets rid of one set of difficulties to create another; but to some of us nothing Dante wrote will ring so full and true as before, and Dante proves himself less of a poet and less of a man than we thought him.

The blending of the symbolic with the historic need not vex us; it is a frequent feature of the poem; Virgil, the symbol of Human Philosophy, is also the courteous poet with honour among poets, the example and master of Statius, Sordello, and Dante in their art. Statius has his symbolic aspect as well as his human life; Cato, too, and St. Bernard are unmistakably historic characters whose human story leads us up to their symbolic significance, and all these contrast with such purely allegorical personages as the

D

lovely nymphs of the vision in the Earthly Paradise, who have no earthly experience of human maidenhood, but have only symbolic attributes, and in heaven are not souls but stars. As to Beatrice, we may argue on either side and find support here or there; it is a question to be decided by feeling rather than argument. Do we feel Dante's works to be just political and philosophical treatises, or are they alive with the individual soul-life of a man to whom the fullest human life was the deepest reality, and to whom every individual experience held an eternal significance? If in the *Vita Nuova* and the *Convivio* we do not feel Beatrice to be a lovely and beloved woman, worshipped and mourned by a poet's heart, I do not think any textual criticism will solve the problem. Apart from the *Vita Nuova* there are of course abundant personal touches. In this canto we have her exclamation, "my friend, but not of fortune"; we have Lucia's reproach, "why helpest thou not him who loved thee so that for thee he left the vulgar throng"; again, we have the words that class her with the other heavenly ladies of whose human reality we are in no doubt, "why art thou not bold and free when three such ladies *vv.* 121-125. care for thee in the Court of Heaven," Virgil says to Dante. The other two are the Blessed Virgin and St^a. Lucia, whose personal and historical reality is untouched by the circumstance that they personify that prevenient grace which comes to help the sinner before he knows his need, and that enlightening grace which makes Lucia's liege man ready for the teaching alike of Virgil, and of Beatrice.

We know from the story of the *Vita Nuova,* *V.N.*, xi. 1-15. how when Beatrice, the pure and gracious Florentine maiden, granted to Dante her salutation no man remained his enemy, but rather a flame of love touched him which caused him to pardon whoever might have offended him, and whosoever should then have asked of him anything he could only have answered with face clad with humility—Love. So, living, she ennobled his youth, and when she talks with him in the Earthly Paradise, her reproach *Purg.*, xxx. 121-141. is that when she changed the earthly for the heavenly life he forgot her, though she was not another, but only more all that might have blessed and uplifted his life. "Some time I sustained him with my countenance; showing my youthful eyes to him I led him with me, turned to the right goal. So soon as I was on the threshold of my second age, and I changed life, he forsook me, and gave him to others. When I was risen from flesh to spirit, and beauty and virtue were increased within me, I was less precious and less pleasing to him; and he did turn his steps by a way not true, pursuing false visions of good, that pay back no promise entire. Nor did it avail me to gain inspirations, with which in dream and otherwise, I called him back; so little recked he of them. So low sank he, that all means for his salvation were already short, save showing him the lost people. For this I visited the portal of the dead, and to him who has guided him up hither, weeping my prayers were borne." Again, when Dante with bitter sighing and weeping says, "Present things with their false pleasure turned away my steps soon as your face was hidden," she replies, "Ne'er did nature and art present to thee pleasure so great as the fair members wherein I was enclosed, and are scattered to dust; and if highest pleasure thus

Purg., xxxi. 34-36, 49-54.

failed thee by my death, what mortal thing ought then to have drawn thee to desire it?"

There is much more in this strain. Finally, she, who in this canto of the *Inferno* is named as sitting with the ancient Rachel in the Paradise of God, is once more, at the close of the vision, placed among the human souls, the daughters *Par.,* xxxi. 70–90. of Eve, at whose feet she sits with Sarah, Rebecca, Judith and Ruth. It is then that we find Dante has fully entered into the true union of souls, and as Beatrice sits aloft and he stands, still separated by his human flesh, he knows that spirit with spirit can meet, and seeing all the lifelong benediction of her guiding, prays that still she will preserve her munificence in him, so that his soul which she has made sound may unloose it from the body pleasing to her.

In the *Inferno* this is our one meeting with Beatrice, and one thing we must notice. Beatrice weeps for Dante's sin; the consummation of bliss is not yet, not till all is perfected on the Resurrection morn: tears are still shed in Paradise, tears of sorrow as of joy. Yet she does not suffer for the misery of the condemned; there are no tears for them.   To Beatrice here, as to Cato later on, these reprobate souls are dead indeed. This is the most terrible aspect of the *Inferno.* Dante could, at least intellectually, believe that evil could everlastingly reign in human souls. For such souls Beatrice, because she is perfectly at one with God, can have no pity.   If we accept the belief we must accept its consequence. Yet Dante pitied to tears, even to fainting, some souls in his own *Inferno.*   He tells us that in the circle of the lovers, when he heard the story of Francesca, " Whilst the one spirit thus spake, the other wept so, that I fainted with pity, as if I had been dying ; and fell, as a dead body falls."

Most certainly we find in Beatrice the fair human maid grown to a perfect beauty in her heavenly home, but also, just as Virgil symbolises the Human Philosophy upon which the ideal Empire should rest, so Beatrice in the *Comedy* symbolises the Divine Science, the Knowledge of God upon which the ideal Church should rest.   We know from the treatise *De Monarchia* that Dante believed the Church ought to teach men that which is essential for them to know in order to attain to the fruition of the Divine Aspect, the blessedness of the Eternal Life. He also believed that had man remained innocent and lived out the true human life of Eden he would have needed neither Pope nor Emperor; he would have been his own Pope and Emperor, sane in mind and heart, perfect in willing obedience, crowned and mitred as Dante was by Virgil when he parted from him in the Earthly Paradise. Truly human, but not fully developed, man would then have needed enlightenment and teaching in Divine things. Eden was an incomplete state, obedience would have won knowledge and the immortal felicity. Dante thought that Man and Angel, Lucifer, who would not wait for light, and Eve, who *Par.*, xix. 46–48. would not remain under the veil, alike fell *Purg.*, xxix. 23–30. immature because they would not accept limitation, partial ignorance, and receive from God a gradual enlightenment. Seeking completion within their own desires and ambitions, they lost their life. Beatrice meets Dante after he attains to the true human freedom, and she represents the Divine Enlightenment which comes to the obedient soul, the Wisdom of God, Theology, or whatever name we give to that teaching which leads to the perfect fruition, the Vision of God.

FROM THE GATE TO THE BURNING CITY

> " Nessun maggior dolore,
> Che ricordarsi del tempo felice
> Nella miseria."   *Inferno*, C. v. 121–123.

> " Maestro," dissi lui, " or mi di' anche :
> Questa Fortuna, di che tu mi tocche,
> Che è, che i ben del mondo ha sì tra branche ? "
> " Quest 'è colei, ch'è tanto posta in croce
> Pur da color, che le dovrian dar lode,
> Dandole biasmo a torto e mala voce.
> Ma ella s'è beata, e ciò non ode :
> Con l'altre prime creature lieta
> Volve sua spera, e beata si gode."
>   *Inferno*, C. vii. 67–69, 91–96.

THE thought of Beatrice, and her love and wisdom, are to Dante's courage what the sunlight, with its life-giving warmth, is to the wild flowers that lift their petals heavenward at the dawn of day.   Everything is possible to him for whom there is loving thought in heaven, and who has at his side the gentle, courteous guide whose words are at once a reproof and an encouragement. Fear is forgotten in action, and Dante starts with fresh resolve on the arduous journey.

Canto iii.

The first step is the step through the gate.

> " Through me is the way into the doleful city;
> Through me the way into the eternal pain;
> Through me the way among the people lost.
> Justice moved my High Maker;
> Divine Power made me,
> Wisdom Supreme and Primal Love.
> Before me were no things created but eternal;
> And eternal I endure: leave all hope ye that enter."

These are the words that Dante reads over the grim portal of Hell, and to us, as well as to him, their meaning is hard. I think we can scarcely doubt that Dante believed that men could so sin and resist the grace of God that they became evil for evermore, and were everlastingly shut out from repentance and hope of the Vision of God. Yet, in the very words which he inscribes over the Gate of Hell, there is a gleam of hope to comfort us at the beginning of our journey, as Virgil's cheerful countenance comforted Dante.

In the first place these words declare that

Justice and Love are one, simply two ways of expressing the same thing : as Love can only be perfected by the triumph of Justice, so Justice can only be fulfilled in the satisfaction of Love. That these can so fulfil one another, and yet evil grow in God's world for ever and ever, seems too illogical a conclusion, and we are driven with Browning's Pope to hope that, in

> "That sad obscure sequestered state
> . . . God unmakes but to remake the soul,
> He else made first in vain; which must not be."

In the second place, when we study Dante's teaching elsewhere, it appears that the word eternal is used in two senses in this passage. Before the gate of Hell only the Eternal Things were made. In the *Paradiso* we are told what *Par.*, vii. 130–148. are the Eternal Things, which were directly created by God and are incorruptible. They are the Angelic Powers and potential matter ; that is to say, not any actual material thing, but that underlying matter from which the actual material things are made, and the force or virtue which informs, that is, gives their form to them. The Universe, as we see it with our earthly eyes, is all corruptible, but not so the heavenly elements, which will go on expressing God's great Idea to all eternity. One other thing comes direct from the heart of the consummate goodness of God, and is made to long for its eternal home. It is the soul of man, and also that body which shall be his soul's expression at the Resurrection, and which shall represent the body God gave to Adam, a perfect divine gift, fit and uncorrupt.

Hell was not, Dante tells us in so many words in the close of the *Inferno*, made directly by God. It was when Lucifer fell, through pride, that in his fall he made the pit of Hell. It was prepared for the Devil and his angels, as it only could be by their own act, not by God for them. Hell, Dante believes, will now endure everlastingly, but he does not say it is in its own nature eternal. It is not part of God's Idea of the Universe.

This second thought, which may be legitimately found in the form of words over the gate, taken along with the later passages referred to, strengthens our gleam of hope, and the light comes from Dante's own teaching, from the Truth as it was expressed in that age. Our hope is that evil, with all other corruptible things, is, however terrible and hideous and far-reaching in its inevitable results, yet but an episode in the development of the Eternal Idea of the Universe. If that is so, the soul of Man, having reaped to the full the sad harvest of his sowing to corruption, will come forth once more reinstated in its life, made able by God, as Dante so beautifully puts it, to up-lift itself again.

That Dante had this hope consciously is, I think, very doubtful, though it is certain that he saw many germs of good and nobility in very many of those whom he met on his sad journey, and that, even in the gloom of the nether Hell, there is some light upon the livid walls; that light can only have come from the sun, the divine source of all light; there is, too, a way out thence into the world of hope and fruitful pain.

However this may be, Dante's thought is not concerned here so much with the measure or duration of evil as with its nature and reality. Dante's thought, and that which weighs heavily on our hearts as we read, is of the inevitable results of an evil choice. The *Inferno* is a most practical poem, and Dante will devote all his strength to drive home the moral truth.

His Master, Virgil, has given us a memorable picture of the lower regions, and he has depicted its guardians as dignified and even grand ; Dante depicts the guardians of the infernal circles of set purpose as coarse and grotesque. Even Minos is a sort of nightmare of the guilty conscience dreaming of its judge. Milton depicts evil passions, such as Pride, Hate, Self-glorification, in his Hell, but the picture is vague in its outlines, and, from the moral point of view, unimpressive compared with Dante's, where the human heart is laid bare, little by little, in its complexity of evil.

Hell is as obedient to God's will as Heaven, for its meaning is Retribution. Here sin bears its certain fruit. If it did not, Justice and Love would not be satisfied. There is no love in letting off the sinner. If we could picture a state where evil brought satisfaction it would be a far more hideous Hell than Dante's. We may indeed be thankful to believe with Anselm, that we cannot escape God's will any more than we can flee from the heavens, to one part of which we approach as we depart from another; we can only shun God's will commanding by subjecting ourselves to God's will punishing.

The thought here is, then, of Retribution, not of Education. All idea of spiritual or corrective punishment is meantime excluded. We are in a materialistic atmosphere. Mental suffering in the *Inferno* is caused by disappointment and defeat, or by fear, or even by loving anxiety for others; it is caused by thoughts of the condition of the beloved native land, or of the party to which the unhappy soul had belonged; it is caused by rage and shame at being found out, that shame which stands at the opposite pole from repentance, but it is never caused by a sense of sin. The state we have to witness is the state of the soul that still chooses evil. Pain is a sign of health in a wounded body, and the safeguard of our physical life. Pain, because of moral evil, is a sign of health in the soul, the safeguard of the moral life. It is always the divine in us that suffers for sin. The extreme instance of this, which brings the truth home to our hearts, is Christ suffering for the sins of His brethren. There the Divine Humanity is united in love to our spoiled humanity, represented by the malefactors at His side. That is the real crucifixion that works salvation for the individual or for the world. In Hell there is nothing of this, the will to do evil is firm and unmoved, and so penitence is excluded, for "it is not possible to repent and will a thing at the same time, the contradiction not permitting it."

Here then, impenitent sin is allowed to make its own atmosphere, that is Hell; here the "Good of the Intellect" is lost. The supreme good of the intellect—what is that? Aristotle calls it Truth; Dante calls it the Vision of God; St. John says it is "To know the only true God and Jesus Christ whom He has sent."

Now we enter the outer regions of Hell. The *Inferno* has its three greater divisions as well as its nine circles and its many subdivisions. This is carefully explained by Virgil later, and here we need only notice that the first region, in which we now are, is, roughly speaking, equivalent to Aristotle's category of Incontinence, that is, of the ill-regulated indulgence of natural desires. Here are the less grievous sinners who are not doomed to the fiery pains suffered within the burning city of Dis. Here we may be surprised to find what we are accustomed to think of as specially gross sinners. We shall understand, as we descend with Dante, how he felt that the malicious sins of the tongue, and the fraudulent use of the intellect, destroy far more completely the image of God in Man, than the grossest carnal indulgence can.

Inside the gate, but outside the circles of *vv.* 39-61. Hell, and on this side the river Acheron, we meet the Coward Neutrals. These are the souls who, carried hither and thither by public opinion, never really lived while on earth ; they never chose, but, standing on one side and making selfish ease their only standard, avoided responsibility. Perhaps, while on earth, they also avoided blame, and were deemed very sensible or amiable persons ; but, when the material surroundings of the external life fell away, the lack of the true soul-life became evident. Now,

E

unclothed by righteous acts, naked and lost to fame, they who dared not face the taunts of men, run hither and thither goaded by the stings of noxious insects. They who failed to hold up the banner of right, or even openly and boldly to stand by any banner, good or evil, in the battles of the earthly life, now follow helplessly the movements of a shifting banner which whirls swiftly along but with no purpose in its movements, no device blazoned on it to command allegiance. Dante, who was so strong and lofty in spirit, and who made a party by himself in face of every faction, felt these cowards more contemptible than many more evidently sinful souls. There is more hope for a man who acts out the evil that is in him than for such as these; when it is seen in the act he may come to loathe and leave his sin, whereas hidden under a specious inoffensiveness he himself may not recognise its very existence. Browning's poem, "The Statue and the Bust," holds the same thought; it is "the unlit lamp and the ungirt loin" that are contemptible in the eyes of both poets who are both strong men and true themselves.

At this point Dante notices a procession of *v. 70.*
souls wending their sad way to the banks of a
river, "the joyless strand of Acheron": Charon
with his boat is ready, and by this Ferry all
souls doomed to the pains of Hell must pass.
By this way no good spirit passes; Dante, with
all penitent souls, will pass by the Tiber to the
unseen world.   This river here girds the whole
realm; it reappears lower down as a black,
boiling fountain, streaming over to form the
Stygian marsh, and again as the blood-red
Phlegethon in the Wood of the suicides; finally,
it flows down to form the frozen lake of Cocytus.
Whatever name it bears, this is the same river;
it is formed by all the tears that have been
made to flow by the evils and miseries of bad
government and human perversity.

Rejected by Charon, but conveyed across *Canto iv.*
the fatal river while unconscious, Dante wakens
to find himself in the blind world, in the first
circle of the Inferno.   Here gloom and darkness
reign, but these do not daunt Dante's spirit, it
is the pallor of his guide that wakens his fears.
Virgil explains that it is not fear that makes
him so pale, but sympathy.   This is the circle *Circle i.*

that claims Virgil as its own ; its chill is in his heart, he shares its loss and hopeless longing. Many and great crowds are here—men and women and children, the unbaptised, and those who before the coming of Christ worshipped not God aright. Men of great worth are here, men who, we learn elsewhere, knew and followed all the cardinal virtues though not clad with Christian Faith, Hope, and Love.

Great sorrow was in Dante's heart because of the teaching of his day. He longed to believe different things as to the Justice of God. His anguish in thinking of the fate of the Heathen grew with the years ; it was a hunger to have the Justice of God made clear. At last the hunger was stilled. He trusted the demand within his heart as of the very nature of the Divine Justice, and in the paradisaic vision he gets the answer. Trajan, the Roman, and Ripheus, the Trojan, shine beyond the shadow of the earth, and, in the heaven of Justice, are two of the great lights that form the eyebrow of the eagle, symbol of justice and righteous government. With regard to Trajan's happy fate, Dante follows the well-known story

of his resuscitation in answer to the prayers of
St. Gregory, his baptism, and consequent salvation; but Ripheus is boldly introduced among
the blessed spirits without any such holy quib-
bling. Faith, Hope, and Love, were to him for
baptism. Cato, we also learn, will at the great *Purg.*, i. 73-75.
day shine forth with the righteous. In his case,
the faithful exercise of the four cardinal virtues,
and a steadfast belief in the immortality of the
soul and in the transcendent value of the life of
the spirit, have saved his soul alive.

Though Dante had this growing hope for
individuals, he yet places here, among those who
sigh without hope, the bulk of his great heathen
teachers. In doing this, the judgment seems
pronounced rather on the limitation of the teaching than on the demerits of the teachers. Certainly in Virgil's case, he who led others to
Christ and who has honour before the Lord of
all is not condemned as an individual soul. I
think we shall not go far wrong if in this circle
we accept the allegorical interpretation which
Dante has told us is the more important. It
then becomes a picture of the soul of man
seeking Truth by his unaided reason, unlighted

by the belief in the direct revelation of the Divine Mind to the human. We recognise the difference between those who grope among the evidences of God's presence to be found in the world around and above, and in the reasonings of the human intellect about them, and those who, with glad realisation, have listened to the voice of Christ declaring, " I and the Father are one," and who, henceforth, have the evidence in their own hearts that God is directly manifesting Himself to them. For them the vision of God has begun already, even as they look into the faces of their brother men.

In this dim region, where Dante would fain have lingered, "honour" sounds forth again and again from his verses. Here are gathered the poets he specially revered; Homer leads the school of this, the Art that is, for Dante, to other arts as the eagle to other birds. This group gathers Dante in among their number, and he shares in their high discourse of lofty themes, not to be repeated to us now. Dante classes himself here with the great poets, as he classed himself before with those who had a great prophetic mission. This is not at all

vv. 72, 73, 74, 76, 80.

inconsistent with his shrinking fears, nor with his repeated hope that others may excel him in the future. The greatness of the message, the possibilities of the art are far more overwhelming to the true prophet, or the true maker, than to the man of small aims and mediocre gifts. He knows that many prophets, many poets must arise before the message can be fully spoken, or the poem perfectly sung.

Apart from the Greek and Roman world of poets, heroes, and philosophers, sits the lonely figure of Saladin. Dante once and again introduces among the many groups of spirits a lonely form, Sordello, who greets him and Virgil as *Purg.*, vi. 58, 59. they approach the Valley of the Kings, and the contemplative English King Henry III. are two *Purg.*, vii. 130–131. of these. There must have been a special touch of sympathy with such in Dante, who himself must so often have been conscious of soul loneliness, moving among the multitude but not of it, singing his great song and leading his life apart.

Out from this serene secluded region, where the pain endured seems but the continuation of a life of thought and dialectic such as these spirits had pursued on earth, with an added note of weariness because the hope of a solution of life's problems has died in them, out into the troubled air, out into a thicker darkness the poets pass.

Canto v.
Circle ii.

We pass with them from the region of limitation to that of conscience of evil. Only now, indeed, do we feel that we have entered Hell proper. On the virtuous heathen no moral condemnation is passed; but here sits Minos, the discerner of sin. He, responding to the self-revelation of the sinner, dooms him to find his torment in that circle for which the condition of his character makes him the fitting denizen. It is a judgment of exact retribution; the awful sentence, " He that is unrighteous, let him do unrighteousness still: and he that is filthy let him be made filthy still."

v. 28.

Dante tells us that this place is void of light. Darkness is the symbol of separation from the true life as the sun is the symbol of God flooding the universe with the light of Truth. Yet we note that there is enough light to see by: no part of God's Universe can exist without some ray of God's light in it.

Human pity is alive in Dante here. If Virgil blanched with sympathetic pain among those who are doomed to fail of the vision of God, Dante's heart melts within him now. He knew the temptations of the sinners tormented here, he shared too their failure; but for the grace of God, and the reawakened thought of the blessed Beatrice, his failure might have been as dire as theirs.

Outside the city of Dis we have no proud boasting of sin, and Dante's pity is always ready. Here there is a poignant personal touch in it as he realises "What sweet thoughts, what *vv.* 113, 114. longing led them to the woful pass."

In this second circle we have those souls who soiled the beauty of love by failure in duty. As they were driven by the winds of passion on earth, so now they are driven helplessly in the hellish storm that never rests. On earth they would enjoy one another in spite of the stern command of duty and loyalty; now they are irrevocably joined together in a pain that is doubled by their union.

Dante does not dwell on the facts of Francesca's story; what he gives us is a picture, lovely and touching, of her heart, of her love and suffering. All his poet nature is awake in the realisation of the pain of lost joy remembered. It is not separation that is the pain, for Francesca and her lover are together. The joy they seized was not of the eternal kind ; it was carnal, fleeting, their loss is spiritual, eternal : the joy that can be all lost is only a misery in remembrance. The love that is spiritual is an eternal joy through all separation. Though *Par.*, xxxi. 73–78. separated farther than is the depth of the sea from the highest heaven, Dante could feel near to Beatrice and still be possessor of the past as of the present love.

Not all his pity for the gentle Francesca, not his condemnation of the treachery that compassed her death, blinds Dante's eyes to the failure of her life. She is chosen out from the multitude of storm-tossed souls, as one who did not bridle the wind of selfish passion on earth, *V. N.* xl. and who must now reap the whirlwind. He who wept till he was blind at the remembrance of his untruth to Beatrice, knew well that the self-indulgence that usurps the name of love is rooted in dishonour, and bears a seed of death.

Overcome by memories, by pity, and by grief, Dante falls in a deathlike swoon, but only to wake to the knowledge of fresh sufferings.

The symbolism of the new circle is easily Canto vi.
Circle iii. read. We have the contrast to the banqueting-hall, where everything is arranged to delight the senses; there sweet scents fill the air, wonderful and mysterious dishes tempt the appetite; witty, it may be learned talk pleases the mind, only the higher nature, the demand of the spirit is put aside: fully to enjoy such a scene, the soul must be lulled to sleep; to live permanently in such a world without remorse brings atrophy to the soul.

Here, guarded by the greedy Cerberus, with his triple throat, hideous and sensual, the spirits wallow amid every miserable discomfort, and breathe in putrefaction; instead of song and laughter we hear only a howling as of dogs. When the lower does not subserve the higher it is mere corruption. This is the test of all gratification, that it minister to a higher growth, to a true and living beauty. Dante feels this a most disgusting circle; surely these are the

poorest things for which a soul can be sold.
No love of man and woman can be without
a touch of the spirit in it; but here is the pure
animal : just the body, food, clothing, the pretti-
nesses that are not beautiful; the Dives-life
that may throw an alms to the beggar, but
gives away its soul for purple and fine linen.
Dante thinks painfully of the nights he spent
with his dear friend Forese Donati, and the
witty Ciacco, whom he meets here.

Ciacco was a well-known wit in Florence,
a diner-out — a club-man, as we should say.
vv. 64-75. With him Dante talks of Florence, and Ciacco
foretells things to come.

It is a story of the strife of factions and of
the double-dealing of Pope and King. From
each and all Dante stands aloof, no doubt one
v. 73. of the two who "are just but are not listened
to there." Again and again it will be brought
home to us as we read that Dante is neither
Guelf nor Ghibelline. He is an idealist for
whom no party has a place, and who holds
to a nobler aim than the leader of faction can
see. He is one of the forerunners who already
dreams of Italy as one in language and in laws,

and for his vision he is ready to suffer, and he will suffer, as will by-and-by be unfolded to him and to us.

At the close of this canto we have Dante's question as to the relation of man's sufferings to the completeness of his nature. Will the *vv.* 103–111. torment of these spirits grow or lessen after the great sentence, or will they be the same as now? It is interesting to note how the great questions that fill Dante's thoughts all through his life are brought up in each part of the *Comedy*. Such are the questions as to the condition of the heathen as subject to God's Justice and Love; the relation of man as endowed with the "treasure of the will" to external circumstances of every kind, and this question of the perfecting of man's powers and sensibilities in the union of soul and body. No modern thinker can insist more than did the mediæval thinker on the completion of man's nature by the union of the physical and the spiritual. St. Bernard says that till man's body is perfected no man can perfectly love God. In a like sense is the answer in the three parts of the *Comedy*. Here, Virgil declares that though the word perfection is out of place in Hell, yet even here when men regain their bodies there will be a greater completeness, and so a fiercer capability of pain.   In the *Purgatorio* we have the beautiful description of how the soul, ever seeking for itself a perfect medium of expression, makes for itself a form which follows its thought and feeling as the flame does the fire.   Finally, in the paradisaic vision, we hear how at last body and spirit being united in a strong and perfect life, fire and flame will be one, and the body, redeemed and quickened, will share and enhance the joy of the soul.

Holding this high discourse of the mystery of man's dual nature, Dante and Virgil move onwards, and where the way descends meet Plutus, the god of wealth.

Thus we are introduced to the realm devastated by the accursed wolf.   Dante's whole treatment of the use and abuse of money is full of interest, and awakens many questions. Carnal love and the indulgence of the body touched Dante to weakness for a time, but the sordid love of money never appealed to him.   He had always seen the evil results of that passion in individual, commercial, national, and ecclesiastical life. Here it is chiefly the individual side of the vice that concerns us; later, among the Usurers, the Simoniacs, the Barrators, and others, we see its other aspects. More and more clearly as we proceed the allegorical significance of the punishments comes out. We stand as witnesses of the inevitable doom of character acquired through evil act and choice.

In the *Convivio* Dante contends against the erroneous opinion that wealth can give nobility. *Conv.. iv. 10 114-120 11, 12.* Riches can neither give nor take away nobility, any more than the stream that flows down in the valley can bend the upright tower that stands above on the hillside. Whether gained by luck or by skill, wealth comes more readily to the man of low aims than to him whose mind is occupied by higher things. When it increases, man's greed increases with it, and betrayed by promises of satisfaction, he grasps at more and more of the base coin, which seems to leave his hands as empty as before. Unsatisfied by what he gains, he yet fears to lose his possessions, and so life grows more restless and full of anxiety: the rich man no longer sleeps quietly, as does the son of toil, but starts at every sound, dreading a robber.

Here the view is somewhat different. If money cannot ennoble the soul it is because in itself it is a neutral thing, therefore we see the souls who lived to hoard or to squander money without aim are obscure beyond recognition. They are engaged in work that is at once most toilsome and most fruitless. Their individuality has evaporated. It is in choosing and specialising with money that individuality grows. Into this dull coin we can, with pains and patience, put a soul and make it beautiful. If we do not it will have its revenge and blur out the life of our soul. There seems little here to choose between Avarice and Prodigality, though it is Avarice that dwells most in Dante's mind as the cause of half the evils of the soul. This Dante feels is the great vice of the clergy, and leads to all manner of hateful acts. The confirmed prodigal, we may note, is usually in the end tainted by the faults of the avaricious. To have the money to consume in useless lavishness he often grudges to those who serve his whims their just wages, and, through selfish spending, the lust of possessing grows and destroys the freehanded generosity which is supposed to be the redeeming virtue of the spendthrift.

As he witnesses this aimless contest, Dante *vv. 67–69.* is moved to fresh questioning. This mocking Fortune, what of her and her delusive gifts? When he was writing the *Convivio* Dante was troubled by the thought of the uncertainties of Fortune with her fickle and careless judgments. He speaks of the unjust blame which *Conv., i. 3.* falls on the victim of Fortune's disfavour, and again, following Aristotle, of how Fortune *Conv.. iv. 11.* favours most the evil and the foolish. Now his point of view is changed. As he considers the Eternal Realities, the results of life, he finds that Fortune is the servant of God as surely *vv. 73–96.* as are the Angels who move the heavenly spheres. Her service is really as beautiful and obeys as just a law as does theirs; she is governed by as true a necessity, and is worthy of as high praise. Indeed, they who most blame her are often the truly favoured ones, and would be thanking her if they had clear eyes to see into life's enigmas. After the event all will understand. We see now how Dante, in his enforced divorce from the active life he loved, in his exile from his beautiful, beloved Florence, in all the bitter experiences of his life, was receiving a beautiful gift from this daughter of God, a gift which he has passed on to us and which, immersed in the life of a Florentine citizen, he would never have received for himself or for us. So it was with his teacher Boethius, in his prison at Pavia; so it was with his successor Bunyan, in his at Bedford; so it has been with many another who has been tempted to revile Fortune for her choicest gifts. Fortune calmly does her work and takes no heed of praise or blame; she turns her wheel with the same serene obedience to the divine will inspiring her as do the Angelic Powers that turn the great wheels of the heavenly system.

Circle v., *vv.* 100–102.

Going down from the circle of the Avaricious and Prodigal, we come to the black, boiling fountain from which Styx, the river of Melancholy, flows. It flows through a cleft in the rock and forms the shallow lake or marsh which is the fifth circle of the *Inferno*, the abode of the souls given over to anger. They live now, as on earth, the uncontrolled life of anger and hate. Many are seen on the surface tearing one another in purposeless rage, while many more, sullen and melancholy, are sunk beneath the slime in loveless gloom. The special offence *vv.* 115-126. of the latter is that when they lived in the sweet air gladdened by the sun they gave no glad response. These morose souls seem akin to the lifeless neutrals on the farther land of Acheron. Lovelessness and idleness are the parents of gloom, and in the gloomy heart jealous anger is apt to usurp the place left empty of loving service. Deprived by circumstance of his share in the busy activity of political life, Dante knew well the temptation to let the heart fill with this lazy smoke, this accidy in which the soul shuts out the light of God's sun, but Dante still triumphed, rejoicing Ep. ix. in the light of heaven as he wrote, with sunny courage, in a moment of great discouragement, to a friend in Florence, that from every corner of the earth he can yet see the sun and the stars.

The guardian of this circle is the furious Canto viii.

Phlegyas; in anger he burned the Temple of Apollo and broke the laws that should govern the dealings of men with their fellows, and so he appropriately leads the children of Pride into the city of rebels, the city of fire. It is here, within sight of the fiery city, that we first, in the person of Filippo Argenti, meet with the mention of pride, and we realise that we shall now sink in the scale of being. Up to this point, we have seen self-indulgence, slavery to the low aim, sordid love of what is dead and deadening to the soul, but now, when pride shows itself, the warping of human nature is aggravated. Filippo seems to gather up in one the carnal sins of this whole division of Hell. Prodigal, having his very horse shod with silver, pompous, of little virtue, arrogant and furiously wrathful, we see him gnawing himself; thus he leads our thoughts on to the bestial degradation towards which we are even now descending. Filippo Argenti was an enemy of Dante's family, and in this meeting Dante gives way *vv. 44, 45.* to arrogant and angry speech. Virgil indeed praises this violent displeasure as a worthy indignation, but I think most of us feel that it is one of the few passages that give some colour to the criticism of those who say that Dante rejoices to put his enemies in Hell. Certainly he here seems touched by the sin of the circle he is in, angry and vengeful, and proud with that pride which had been the bane *Par.*, xv. 91–96. of his family, and which made him fear when *Purg.*, xiii. 133–138. he thought of the first torment of the Purgatorial Mount.

THE CITY OF DIS

Suo cimitero da questa parte hanno
Con Epicuro tutti i suoi seguaci,
Che l'anima col corpo morta fanno.

Inferno, C. x. 13–15.

Non ti rimembra di quelle parole,
Con le quai la tua Etica pertratta
Le tre disposizion che il ciel non vuole ;
Incontinenza, malizia e la matta
Bestialitade? e come incontinenza
Men Dio offende, e men biasimo accatta?

Inferno, C. xi. 79–84.

Canto viii.

PHLEGYAS comes across the marshy lake in obedience to a signal by flame from a great tower on its farther side. He is furious because the passengers awaiting him are not his lawful prey, but he consents to ferry them to the gates of a city which glows on the inner margin of the marsh.

Weighed down by the unusual burden of one still bearing his mortal body, his boat makes *vv.* 31-39. the return voyage somewhat slowly, and it is in its course that the conversation with Filippo Argenti takes place.

Dante's attention is soon all absorbed in what lies before him. Through the dark, foggy air mosque-like towers glow out red, like hot iron. This, Virgil tells Dante, is the City of Dis. In the *Æneid* the place of torment bears this name, and we are now repeatedly told that we are entering the lowest Hell. Everything impresses us with the sense of deeper guilt, of heavier penalty within these gloomy walls, with their lurid towers filled with malicious and furious demons.

Up to this point we have not descended much ; henceforth we sink to ever lower depths. Many fallen angels are here in the region of Pride ; they had no place among those who were mere slaves of the senses. This city is ruled from below, where its master has his throne. Pride, which on earth tempts men to think themselves great and noble, has its throne in the lowest abyss of Hell. These fallen angels, bent on the work of destruction, realise they have no immediate power over Dante, they must trust to his mere human folly to compass his undoing. Meantime, they think Virgil may be detained by force or fraud.

Dante is overcome by fear when he hears the threats of the demons, but Virgil brings him now, as so often, the message of hope. Be of good hope, he tells him, and it is a fitting exhortation here at the portals guarded by the servants of Despair. God's will is Dante's sanctification, and that through the accomplishment of this journey, and it will be accomplished. The bad angels have no power over Virgil, but neither can he force an entrance. The gate is shut in his face, and he returns to Dante. White with anger, rather than with fear, he reminds Dante how they once before, but vainly, withstood Christ at the Gate of Entrance, and assures him that at this gate Christ's Angel will overcome.

Canto ix. If not afraid, Virgil is at least confused and disturbed, and doubts awaken in Dante's mind as to his leadership; he questions him as to former experiences, and Virgil reassures Dante as to vv. 25-30. his knowledge of the way. He penetrated once to the darkest recess of Hell, the spot farthest from the heaven of life-giving energy. Dante can remember little of what Virgil told him, for once more the city draws all his thought to itself. The angels have, perhaps, withdrawn within, at least they are forgotten in the awful sight that now greets him. The Furies stand out on the flaming tower, and they are the proper guardians of the city. The handmaidens of Proserpine, furious and vengeful, they bewail the escape of Theseus from their clutches, and hope this time to make sure of a victim by the aid of Medusa, who will turn Dante to enamel, more hard than stone, fused by searing fire. They, the evil avengers, are evidently symbolic of that hopeless remorse which leads to despair, the very opposite of penitence. Well might St. Benedict end his Rule with the exhortation : " Never despair of the goodness of God." Penitence is the sorrow of the child turning to his father to be put right ; remorse is a dwelling in the thought of sin which brings despair of any putting right. Despair is the absolute unbelief ; to despair is to be an atheist. As long as God is the centre of our Universe the right can be accomplished, hope cannot die.

Rightly then, the Furies are represented as

calling on Medusa. If Dante can be forced to gaze upon the very face of evil, his soul will die within him. Virgil, the prophet of hope, cannot open the gate; he cannot, by his philosophy, overcome the spirit of doubt and unbelief, but he can save Dante from despair while they wait for the heavenly messenger *vv. 55-60.* bringing grace from on high. In very tender words Dante tells how the Master turned him from the freezing horror, and as he covered his eyes at his command, put his hands over those of his trembling disciple to make him doubly safe from the vision of evil. The contemplation of essential evil is fatal to the life of the soul, and to overcome it grace from on high is needed. *vv. 61-63.* We know that we do well to seek a spiritual meaning in this passage, for Dante tells us that a deep teaching is to be found underlying the words.

vv. 64 sqq. As they stand, hoping and fearing, angry and expectant, the promised angel is heralded by a rushing sound, as a multitude of the spirits of the marsh scatter and flee before his face, as broken branches flee before a gale. This is the only angel we meet in the Inferno, and he is very literally only a messenger; silent, disdain-ful, unbending, untouched by the evil powers that flee before him, breathing with loathing the thick, foul air of this place, he fleets dry-shod over the marsh, waving aside the hateful fog with his left hand. Dante bows before him, but he pays no heed to Dante or to Virgil; his errand has all his thoughts. With brief, scorn-ful words he rebukes the rebellious demons, and with a touch of the wand that he carries in his right hand he opens the gate; then, intent on the next behest of his Lord, he gladly returns by the way he came.

Within the walls we are in a strange city. Canto x. Circle vi. It is a city of the dead. On either hand stretches a great plain, all uneven with tombs. No doubt this is a reminiscence of Arles, where are long rows of Roman tombs, and where Charlemagne's soldiers were supposed to have been buried after the battle of Roncesvalles. On some of those tombs there were inscriptions, as on some here; but here there is a horror unknown in any quiet earthly resting-place of the worn-out body. These tombs glow with fire. The black country of the Midlands, with its blazing furnaces glowing in the darkness of night, has been suggested as a picture like this of the fiery tombs of the city of Heretics.

The position and condemnation of Heretics at the beginning of a new section of the Inferno, attracts our attention, and leads us to consider Dante's classification of sins and his attitude to the Spirit of Doubt.

In the *Inferno* the classification of sins may, in a general sense, be said to be founded on that of Aristotle in the *Ethics*. This gives us a division into three parts: i. Incontinence; the sins of wrong or excessive use of things good in themselves, sins of impulse. ii. Bestiality; the morbid love of things not good in themselves, habits contrary to nature, brutish sins. iii. Malice; the fiendish sins, sins which signify the degradation of Man's highest part, his Reason, the perversion of human nature. Dante does not use these precise names, but the Violence of Circle vii. is very like Aristotle's Bestiality; and Fraud, punished in Circles viii. and ix., includes all abuse of specifically intellectual faculties. Questions arise; many of the sins are hard to place; viewed from one side they seem to belong to one category, from another one to a different one. One explanation helps us somewhat in this difficulty. As we descend we do not merely meet with different sins, but with added sinfulness ; the robber adds cunning to violence, the seducer adds treachery to incontinence.

In the *Purgatorio* the classification is more directly that of the Church. This is natural, as the souls are represented as submissive to Church discipline. Heresy does not appear, *Purg.*, iii. 139–141. but he who is excommunicated by the Church must wait thirtyfold the time he hath lived in his presumption.

Equally outside the view of Aristotle are the Non-belief or imperfect belief of Limbo, and the Heresy of the sixth circle, but they are appropriately placed by Dante. At the entrance, apart from the morally culpable, but deprived by their limited, earth-bound philosophy of the full Vision of God, are the non-believers, those who do not attain ; here, between the incontinent and the bestial, but more akin to the latter, are those who deny. Dante's attitude towards heresy must greatly interest us. The greatest intellect of his day, none was a deeper believer than Dante, yet he was a keen questioner and most certainly no upholder of mere Authority as such ; we wish therefore to find, if possible, what it is that he so sternly condemns in this circle.

Conv., ii. ix. If we look at Dante's teaching in the *Convivio* we find there that he looks upon the denial of the immortality of man's spiritual part as the most vile and hurtful bestiality. This denial is contrary to the demand of our intellect. To gain the eternal life men have willingly sacrificed the physical life, and he feels if it has been a vain sacrifice we are indeed miserably deceived. Again, let us see what Dante says of man's *Par.*, iv. 26, questionings in the *Paradiso*. There we find 27, 64-69. more light shed on the subject. Two questions have arisen in his own mind, and one Beatrice declares to lead to a more poisonous error than the other. This question is as to the relation of man's soul to the stars, and the error combated is that the souls of men belong to the different stars, and return each to its home at death. This turns the worship of men from God to the gods of the planets. Dante constantly returns to the subject of the influence of the stars on Man's destiny. He believes in this influence, "the honour and the blame of their influence," but it is deadly error to believe that they so bend the Will of man as to relieve him of responsibility. Man's will and God's grace are independent of all external influence. On the other hand, to question deeply as to God's justice is not condemned; it is a less poisonous error. Indeed, it is the sense of justice within us that is our most divine posses-sion, and we show ourselves children of God when we demand that He satisfy our standard of right dealing. The more deeply we ques-tion, the nearer to truth we shall come; only the questioning must not be rooted in pride or in despair, but in humility, and in the hope that for every divine problem there is a divine solution. At the foot of every truth there *Par.*, iv. 130–132. springs a question. If the mind is alive it will question, and only as it questions does its life grow and deepen. Dante never condemns intellectual mistakes. He speaks in one place of a soul laughing in heaven over the mistakes of earth, never of any punishment for such error.

What, then, is the deadly error or heresy of
C. x. 13-15. this circle? Here, Dante tells us are Epicurus
and all his followers. This is not of course a
judgment on the personal life of the great
philosopher, who was as little a voluptuary as
any Stoic; Dante puts Epicurus here because
he believes his teaching led to the materialisation of life. The heresy hateful to Dante is
that proud materialism which denies or sub-
ordinates the spiritual element in man, and
which declares life to have its end and meaning
apart from God. This is an unnatural life; it
is akin to the brute life, and from it will spring
morbid evils, violence, and fraud. When we
meet and converse with the souls placed here,
this view is confirmed. The Heretics are here
fulfilling the conditions adjudged by themselves
while on earth. They believed in death, and
now they are shut up in burning tombs in a
living death. They are shut away from the
Universal Life, and when they regain their
bodies at the judgment-day, their doom will
be completed. Each will be shut within the
tomb, eternally alive, yet spiritually dead

Without Faith and Hope there may be a keen intellectual life, but no real life of the soul.

Here the Pagan materialism of nominal Christians is displayed. The spirit of the early Renaissance, and especially the Court of Frederick II., is in Dante's mind. There a high intellectual life went hand in hand with a sensual materialism in which the life of the soul died. Frederick II. himself is here, the brilliant scholar, the bold crusader who entered Jerusalem but was fain there to set the crown on his own head, because no priest would recognise his kingship. His dissolute life, given over to sensual delights, set the seal to his contempt for the spiritual hopes he denied; a contempt shared by the crowd represented here as his followers.

If the wish which Dante concealed, lest he should vex Virgil by too great impatience, was to know if he should meet some fellow-citizen, it was soon granted, for Farinata degli Uberti, hearing his Tuscan speech, is the first among the entombed to accost him. Farinata's fate had interested Dante when he was among the gluttons, and he questioned his fellow-townsman

v. 18; Cf. iii. 72–81.

G

Ciacco about him, speaking of him as very worthy of honour. He was a Ghibelline and a great lover of Florence, and his son Lapo was a friend of Dante. But love of Florence and hostility to the Pope are not salvation. Farinata was an Epicurean, given up to the joys of a material existence. He was one who shared the brilliance, and was tainted by the evil influence of Frederick's Court; he had denied the claim of the spiritual life.

When Farinata was fighting on the Ghibelline side in 1248, and again at Montaperti in 1260, Dante's family, which was of the Guelf faction, was on each occasion exiled ; but Farinata died in 1264, and Dante's family must have returned the second time to Florence before 1265, when Dante was born there. When Dante wrote this passage he was exiled as a Ghibelline, or at least as an opponent of the methods of the Papal party. Dante's view was a wider one than was possible to the champions of faction. To gain the freedom of all, and to give all possible rights to the free citizens, which the Guelfs claimed as their aim, was not less Dante's ideal than it was theirs, but he thought to gain this end through the pacifying action of the Emperor, who was to rule all with an equal justice. Farinata had this in common with Dante, that he loved Florence more than faction or than revenge, for he saved it from destruction when, after the battle of Montaperti, his party demanded it should be razed to the ground. To those who think that Dante put in Hell those who were his opponents on earth, it should be interesting to note, that while Farinata is in the City of Dis, Provenzan Salvani, who called loudly for the destruction of beautiful Florence at Montaperti, is among the fortunate souls in Purgatory.

Close beside Farinata another Tuscan spirit *vv.* 52–72, 109–114. desires speech with Dante. Cavalcante Cavalcanti interests us because he is the father of Dante's greatest friend, Guido Cavalcanti. He recognises Dante and expects to see his son; he cannot think of the one as far distant from the other. To Guido the *Vita Nuova* was dedicated by Dante; it is possibly to him *Purg.*, xi. 97. Dante refers as a greater poet than Guido Guinicelli; lovely sonnets tell of their affection, all their tastes and interests drew them together. Yet the friends were for some reason alienated. It seems as though when Dante turned to Virgil, and was led by him to the teaching of Aristotle and Boethius, Guido *vv. 61-63.* did not sympathise. It is not, Dante says, thanks to his own genius, that he can face this journey, but led by a higher teaching, and Guido had disdained that aid. It seems that Dante feared that the taint of Epicureanism which lay darkly on the father had touched the son also. The Cavalcanti were of the Guelf party, but Dante, with the other Priors, had in this very year, 1300, banished Guido, with other leaders of that and of the Ghibelline faction, and though Guido still lived at the date of the poem, he died that autumn from illness due to the unhealthy climate in which his exile was passed.

While Dante, only half attentive, speaks with Cavalcante, Farinata is absorbed in his own thoughts. Cavalcante's private sorrows do not touch him. Family pride and the love of *vv. 76-78.* Florence are still his master passions. That his kindred should be hated and exiled pains him more than the torments of Hell, and he tries to solace himself by prophecies of Dante's coming exile and distress. Ciacco had foretold the defeat of the party to which Dante belonged, and now Farinata foretells Dante's personal share in that defeat. Later, Vanni Fucci reiterates the prophecy of banishment as an angry threat.

All the doomed spirits have some dim vision of the future. The life of the senses is closed, and what is at the moment happening on earth is hidden from them, but they are not quite shut from the universal life in God, and see the future which is present in the thought of God. When Time ends and all is fulfilled, they will be completely isolated and shut in to their own miserable individual existence, without part or lot in the great spiritual life that will then absorb past, present, and future in one. Dante is full of wondering at their knowledge, and of questioning as to his own part in the future, but Virgil assures him all will be made clear when he meets Beatrice. As a matter of fact it is not *Par.*, xvii. Beatrice, but Cacciaguida, Dante's own ancestor, who fully unveils the story of Dante's life-sufferings, and justifies him as poet, patriot, and prophet, purging him from all the accusations so often brought against him still, of evil motive in what he wrote against evil men.

Canto xi.   Now, on the edge of a cliff-like descent, the poets pause, driven back by the noisome vapours, and wait till their senses get used to the stench. Every indication is here that we are going down to more hateful moral conditions, and we, like Dante, are keen to learn the wherefore of the darker doom of those whom we are now to visit.

Beneath, Virgil tells, are the Violent and the Fraudulent; at first we are inclined to wonder why some sins are placed so low. When we look into the matter we understand better. Outside the Red City, are only sins of abuse and excess in desires and acts natural and lawful in themselves, and they are sins that cause little pride in the sinners. Now we begin to see human nature degraded and distorted. Among the Violent we have a disregard for the orderly, beneficent working of nature; there we have those who have despised the gift of life and destroyed themselves in wantonness or despair;

those who have distorted the natural human relations and followed a sterile and degraded vice ;
those who have denied their highest human privilege and blasphemed God in proud and rebellious
egoism. We also find there the Usurers, and
Dante feels some explanation of their presence
in that place is necessary. They, too, are sinning against a beneficent natural law, the law
of labour and the privilege of Art.

In the Middle Ages all lending of money for
interest was condemned by the Church. Dante
apparently assents to this judgment, as he seems
to identify usurers with bankers ; Cahors, the
great banking centre of the time, is marked out
for reprobation. This age will not join in that
estimate ; Ruskin has found few to follow him
in his wholesale condemnation of money-lend-
ing. Nevertheless, the principle proclaimed by
Dante as lying at the root of this judgment is
a great one. It goes deep into the real question
of what is essential if the commerce and the
social life of any age is to be sound and wholesome.

We are meant, Dante tells us, to be imitators
of the glad Creator ; we are to be makers, not

all poets in word, but all in action. Our skill is akin to the creative power of God, it is the *v.* 105. "grandchild of the Deity," and we are to use it to add something to the beautiful and useful things of the world. It is the blessed lot of man to labour, and he cannot get away from the responsibility of his humanity. "We receive our life only that we may work for ourselves and for others, and whoso dispenses himself from this sacred duty bears the punishment of Nature in want or in ennui."[1] Surely this is not less true in the twentieth century than in the fourteenth. The mere breeding of money is a poor thing. If we have money without our own labour, it is payment beforehand for work we are meant to do; also we are bound to recognise that our money is part of our power of personal service, we must see to it that it is employed in some way that brings benefit to others. No investment perfectly satisfies the standard of true socialism if by it we only gain our livelihood, we must also *v.* 103. benefit the nation. How difficult not to trans-

[1] Florian.

gress this law, but in contending with the difficulty we are keeping our souls alive.

Below these bestial souls who are less than human, are placed the Fraudulent in the two lowest circles; of such there are many subdivisions. The cunning desire to overreach others may enter into every relation of life and ruin it. In the eighth circle are those who thus destroy the ordinary relations of life, defrauding those who have the common claim of a common humanity, but, lowest of all, frozen and dead to the core, are the base souls who deceive and betray those who have special cause to trust them. These are traitors to country, to kindred, and to just lords and benefactors.

Now Dante recalls our thoughts to the Upper Hell, asking why what seemed so foul and bitter there is not punished within the fiery city. He is easily convinced by Virgil that Aristotle gave a just judgment in this matter. The sinners of the Upper Hell have taken a poor thing in exchange for their true life; they have fallen lower than their human privilege, but they have not called good evil, and evil good. Far more vile are the sins of the spirit. In them God's highest gift of Reason is turned directly against all for which it was given. Man, made in the image of God, has turned that image into the semblance of a fiend. Even to sink to the level of the brutes is a lesser evil than to degrade genius to the service of cunning, to turn love into an instrument of treachery. To betray confidence and to deny the claim of gratitude is to have the ice of the Lake of Hell already in the heart.

THE VIOLENT AGAINST NATURE

THE BLOODY RIVER—THE HORRIBLE WOOD
THE BURNING SAND

> Io pensai che l'universo
> Sentisse amor, per lo quale è chi creda
> Piu volte il mondo in caos converso.
>
> *Inferno*, C. xii. 41–43.

> " O Capaneo, in ciò che non s'ammorza
> La tua superbia, sè' tu più punito :
> Nullo martirio, fuor che la tua rabbia,
> Sarebbe al tuo furor dolor compito."
>
> *Inferno*, C. xiv. 63–66.

> Se tu segui tua stella,
> Non puoi fallire al glorioso porto.
>
> *Inferno*, C. xv. 55, 56.

AS we enter a new region we encounter a Canto xii. new guardian. The guardian of each circle has a symbolic fitness. The greedy Cerberus, Plutus, the god of wealth, the proud and furious Phlegyas, guard the Gluttonous, the Avaricious and Prodigal and the Angry spirits.

The handmaidens of remorse and despair greet us at the entrance to the realm of materialistic denial, and now we see the Minotaur, unnatural in origin, in form, and in habits, gnawing himself in bestial rage, as the fitting ruler over those who have lost their manhood in an unnatural life, or refused to bear their human burden, choosing rather a coward's death. Virgil's contest for a passage also varies at each fresh descent. Here he simply leaves stupid rage, blinding and destroying judgment, to defeat its own ends while he and Dante move quietly forward.

vv. 28-45. The descent here is steep and difficult; the earthquake of the night of the Crucifixion caused the confusion of fallen rocks, among which the pilgrims are now taking their painful way. Virgil recalls an old experience and his sensations then; he says he thought the universe was shaken by love, which, as some believe, always brings chaos. This refers to the teaching of Empedocles, who taught that the state of the world at any time, in its changing phenomena, arises from a partial discord. When Love enters in, it produces a unification of the atoms, bringing about a seeming chaos, out of which a new order arises. This view seems to have attracted Dante. To him the earthquake on the night of our Lord's crucifixion is indeed an evidence of love, shaking the Universe to its centre, and bringing a new order of things into its temporal life. On the Mount of Purgatory an earthquake is the evidence of a great spasm of joy and love, felt by all when a soul is freed from evil, and, renewed in heart and will, mounts toward Heaven.

The thought is an alluring one, for love does, again and again, as it enters life, break up the old conditions, set free new forces, and prepare a new cosmos which shall in its turn be shaken, and make way for yet new workings of the Divine Power that is behind all the changing phenomena of our mortal life.

Once more we come upon the river of Hell ; Circle vii. now it appears as Phlegethon, the boiling, bloody stream which flows entirely round this circle. It is a fitting symbol of the condition of those who violently rejected obedience to God and the restraining law of Nature; now they endure that violent and fruitless existence which they chose.

At the root of all the crimes of violence lies Cupidity; the lean and hungry wolf has her prey in this circle and in all the nether Hell.

In the first division of this tripartite circle those who were violent against their neighbours have the Centaurs as their rulers. Half man, half horse, the Centaur typifies true humanity *Purg.*, ix. marred by the wild passions of the brute. Chiron, 34–39. the least brutal of his tribe, trained Achilles in heroic deeds; Nessus, with false assurances of its virtue to restore her lover to her, gave to Deianira the shirt, stained with his blood, which was to cause the death of Hercules and so avenge his own death; of Pholus we know little but that he is spoken of as furious. In the three we have a descending scale, from the strong, genial animality of Chiron, down to the sheer ferocity of Pholus. In none of them is there a mad bestiality as in the human spirits. *vv.* 97–99. These creatures are not such from choice; they seem quite willing to serve the good, and Chiron readily sends Nessus as guide when he hears that Dante is sent by God, and that Virgil is acting in obedience to the Divine Will and supported by Divine strength.

Here, plunged in the bloody river up to the Girone i. eyebrows, are the Tyrants. They are sunk deeper than others. Here, as elsewhere, Dante takes great examples, "smiting most upon the *Par.*, xvii. 133–142. loftiest summits," that so he may awaken the attention of his hearers and arouse their consciences. Alexander the Great is here a supreme type of the cruelties executed, and miseries caused, through lust of power. Dante, who, more than most men, worshipped authority worthily exercised, saw in tyranny that degradation of the best which is the worst. Else- *Conv.*, iv. 11 123–125 where he praises Alexander for his munificence, but that shows no real inconsistency ; in this, as in many other instances, it is the type more than the individual that is to be considered. Coming nearer home, the individual is more present to our minds as we gaze on the swarthy Azzolino, the Ghibelline ruler of Romano whom Symonds calls " Child of the Devil." He was son-in-law to Frederick II., a wretch, guilty of the most inhuman atrocities, who, when at the last taken prisoner, refused food for many days, and tearing open his wounds, died as he had lived—furious, brutal, and hideous.

vv. 115-120.

Less heinous in their offence, and plunged less deeply in the river, are the Homicides. Separate from the others, one of the lonely figures of the poem, is Guy de Montfort, son of the heroic Simon, who, to avenge his father's death at Evesham, slew his cousin Henry at the most solemn moment of the Mass in the church at Viterbo. This is one of the few references to English history, and perhaps it is as one of a strange race that De Montfort is set apart from the other spirits, as Henry III. sits alone in the Valley of the Kings.

vv. 121-139.

Still less deeply immersed are violent robbers, soldiers, and highwaymen.

Canto xiii.,
Girone ii.

Nessus has performed his task, and having put Virgil and Dante across the ford, he returns to his fellows, while the poets pass into the dreary and unwholesome wood of the suicides. All here is weird and unnatural; the trees are warped, and poisoned, and unreal. Break a twig, and you find it alive with a life that was human once, but is deformed into a lower thing. These wretched beings rejected the human life God gave them. They found it too hard to be men, and craved release, though the fight was not fought to the end. Perhaps they envied the irresponsible life of those lower in the scale of nature, and now they inherit this lower life, but not its natural beauty and peace. They are doomed to suffer penalties possible only to humanity, yet as trees they are exposed to the assaults of the Harpies, who, hideous, dehumanised women, half birds of prey, tear and destroy those quivering branches among which they have their nests. They, like the Centaurs but more vile, typify at once the bestial possibilities of human nature and the Nemesis of remorse.

Among these spirits is one of the noblest *vv.* 31-75. characters whom we meet in the *Inferno*, Pier delle Vigne. Poet and statesman, he was for years Chancellor to Frederick II. Dante's abhorrence for that court, which contained the brightest intellects and nourished the basest life of the period, is shown clearly in this picture of a faithful and able man, done to death by the envy and malice of place-hunters, who used falsehood and slander to compass their ends. Pier declares, what was evidently Dante's conviction, that he had striven always

H

for his master, and never had an unfaithful thought of him whom he still regards as worthy of honour. He could stand proof against temptations to harm his master, but was not strong to bear the shame of imprisonment, the bitterness of exile and of blindness. No Lady of Philosophy came to his rescue with the assurance that nobility, and even happiness, could not be touched by the machinations of evil men, and he dashed his head against a wall, and so died miserably.

We are in a region where acts, now bearing their fruits, are traceable to Pride and Envy. Envy is here specially declared by Dante to be the common bane and vice of courts. To this our Chaucer has set his seal, quoting this passage in the Prologue to his *Legende of Goode Women.*

v. 84.   Great pity is in Dante's heart for the great, earnest soul, whose fate, as the victim of envy, he feels is like his own, and well has he fulfilled the desire of Pier to have the fame of his faithfulness restored on earth.

vv. 103–108.   Only these souls, among all in Hell, will not be reinstated in their bodies at the Resurrection.

They would not bear the burden of humanity, and now they may not resume the human form, but will for ever be reminded of what they once were, while forced passively to bear the lower lot; neither true men nor truly trees, they bear the penalty of an unfulfilled destiny.

As Dante reflects on these things, fresh spirits *vv.* 109-151. rush wildly on the scene pursued by hideous black bitches, which perhaps represent the creditors from whom they had vainly fled through the gate of death. Paduan and Sienese spendthrifts, they had doubly destroyed their life, first squandering what might have been nobly used, then fleeing from the life out of which they had lost all they cared for.

Sorrowfully, Dante accedes to the petition of an unknown fellow-citizen, and gathering up the scattered leaves torn off by another spirit in his agony, lays them by that bleeding bush which imprisons the soul of the Florentine; then he passes on his way.

There is no sadder place in Hell than this Canto xiv. new region. Arid burning sand stretches in a Girone iii. dead desert waste. Here are those who refused the natural relationships of human life, indulging in a sterile and degrading vice; here too are those who refused to see in the gifts of nature and the discipline of life the love and wisdom of the Great Giver, but in proud egoism cursed God and died; those too who saw in beneficent labour only a curse, and would not add their sheaf of grain to the world's harvest-field. All now reap as they have sown. They would not submit themselves to the gracious laws of their natural life, as children of God bringing forth fruit in its season, and now they lie, scorched and deadened, under the fiery rain of Hell which seres and dehumanises, producing nothing. In this sand Dante may not set his feet, but walks along the edge, gazing intently on this new and terrifying spectacle.

vv. 25-27.   Those who directly blasphemed God are comparatively few. Then, as now, there were few who would deliberately call themselves Atheists.

vv. 49-72.   Dante chooses a Pagan soul as the type of the proud Atheist. We often feel as though Dante thought of the gods and goddesses of antiquity as real personages, but again, as here, they represent the revelation to men of old of the same creative, directive, and governing power more fully revealed to the Christian. To defy Jove is to defy all that Capaneus knew of God. Pride is full-fledged here, and finds its true place. The life of egoistic independence is death in life, and now is seen in its impotence of rage and spite. That he now exists apart from the Divine aid and grace, and has pride as his eternal portion, is the inevitable punishment of Capaneus, as one who said on earth that he would stand or fall alone. Later he is coupled with Vanni Fucci as the proudest spirit in Hell. This is one of Dante's central thoughts. Hell's foundations are laid in pride. To separate the soul, as pride alone can separate it, from God, to put God out of all that might be highest in life, keeping it otherwise entire in intellectual life, that is Hell. To call light darkness and darkness light is the eternal sin; the sin that no forgiveness can blot. Few are intellectually Atheists, but anyone who denies God in conscience, calling wrong right against knowledge, has for his punishment just this, that what he was he remains. Pride in evil shuts the door upon repentance. All sin, acknowledged to be sin, can be forgiven, but only the spiritual fire can destroy this.

vv. 76-78.

To avoid the burning sand the pilgrims were still walking on the margin of the wood, and just here a rivulet, running down from it and across the sandy waste, attracts Dante's attention, and he notices its blood-red colour and also its hard, cool margins that pointed it out as a place where they could walk so as to cross to the next descent. There was more here than met the eye, and Virgil tells Dante that this stream is the most notable thing he has yet seen. This surprises Dante, and always keen to learn all he may, he begs Virgil to explain.

vv. 103-120.

Virgil tells that all the streams of Hell, of which this is the third, are really one in their source. In the Isle of Crete, once fertile and beautiful, now wasted and forsaken, on Mount Ida, stands a great statue, which Virgil describes. It is all, except the golden head, rent and broken, and from the rents there flows down a stream of the world's tears to form the gloomy river of Hell. This figure with the golden head, its arms and breast of silver, its lower trunk of brass, and its legs of iron mixed with clay, can be variously interpreted as to details. The Golden Age may be that of Saturn or of the early Roman Empire; the foot of clay may or may not be the Church weakened by earthly alloy from the fatal gift of Constantine. Dante probably thought of the statue as representing the History of the Roman Empire; Damietta would then stand for the old Eastern Monarchies, and the Isle, which was the cradle of the Trojan, and so of the Roman race, would represent the modern civilisation, the Western and progressive world. In any case, it represents the course of human history and its moral significance. This is the notable thing. Virgil would lead Dante to see in all history the working of God's power and moral law. Through Virgil Dante comes to believe in a revelation through history. Men were accustomed to look at Jewish history in this way; as they read the Hebrew Scriptures they said God commanded, or upheld, or punished: Dante says all history is one, there is no chasm. All human, all national life, has its strength in righteousness; the issues of life to-day, as in Jerusalem, are moral issues. Hell is watered and tormented by the evils that flow from the degradation of Government, temporal and spiritual.

To many of us this does seem one of the most notable things that Dante saw. To realise that God is working as really in all history, even in that of our own day, as ever he worked in Moses' day, or David's day, or Hezekiah's, is to realise one of the greatest and most stimulating truths accessible to man.

One personal touch we notice. Dante is always tempted to put the Golden Age in the past all through the poem. Even in the *Paradiso*, though he is hoping for new heroes, a Henry VII. or a Can Grande, to work out God's Will, it is to bring back something of the past glory. The simplicity of the past attracts the poet, but for the Christian the Golden Age must always be in the future. Dante does hope that Christ is working in the abyss, that He has not forgotten the world He came to redeem, but sometimes he fails of the glad confidence of those who believe that the coming, the presence, of Christ is always near, and that therefore good and better days are always coming.

Meantime the river of woe flows on, and this

rill is a branch of Phlegethon that flows down, sinking into the frozen lake of death that Dante has yet to visit. Its secret will, ere long, be revealed. Where then, asks Dante, is Lethe, that other river of the spiritual world? Not here, Virgil replies; here is no water of forgetfulness; that flows only where sinners may wash when penitence has done its cleansing work.

Walking on the firm margin of the rill, they can now cross the burning desert, and fresh forms of evil meet their view. Canto xv.

If few, like Capaneus, directly defy God, many, then as now, do so indirectly, living contrary to Nature's law of love and labour which is God's voice, speaking His claim to the moral allegiance of their hearts.

Defended from the fiery rain by the sheltering smoke of the rivulet, and walking on its hard margin, Dante and the Master hurry on till one of this new crowd of sinners, peering vv. 23-124. through the dismal exhalations of the river, recognises Dante, and in wonder mingled with affection, holds him by the skirt. No sadder meeting than this takes place on all the journey.

Brunetto Latini, born in 1210, had passed the prime of life when Dante was born, and was not his tutor as is sometimes said, but he was one who had led his thoughts towards the life that endures, and had he lived, would have cheered Dante's hard path with the stimulus of intellectual sympathy and fatherly affection. He died in 1294, but the memory of his kind and good influence lives in Dante's heart, and in loving reverence Dante bows down that he may be on a level with this friend of happier days.

vv. 55-78. Their talk is still of the things of the mind, and Brunetto cheers Dante on toward the attainment of noble ends. Like Ciacco and Farinata, he prophesies troubles to come, but his words are on a higher level. It is for his good deeds that Dante will suffer, and such suffering is no real shipwreck ; if he but follow his star he will *Par.*, xxii. yet gain a glorious haven. He must be worthy 110-120. of the star of genius and wisdom, and cleanse himself from the sins of Florence, and all will be well.

In an earthly sense, this prophecy was never fulfilled. Rejected still by Florence and its factions, Dante died as he had lived, poor and

an exile.   Near the end of his life's work, *Par.*, xvii. 103-111.
Dante had many fears of failure, many doubts.
All he seemed likely to gain was the enmity of
the many, though, perhaps, one or two tender
consciences might be touched and awakened by
his burning words.   Yet the haven was gained
in the sense the guide of his youth had taught
him to care most for ; it was gained in the true
fame that is the fruit of the high endeavour
that makes man eternal.   Now the poet does
live, and will live, among those who call his
times ancient.

The whole passage throbs with strong personal feeling ; the lofty thoughts, Dante's strong
readiness to face all that Fortune may bring,
the pathos of Brunetto's loving interest in his
pupil's noble future from out his own spoiled,
withered life, Dante's pain and love, and, withal,
his stern reprobation of evil, which leads him
to doom to such a fate the man he reverenced,
all move us deeply.   Not all Brunetto's lofty
intellectual views had saved his life from the
dark stain of vice, and not all Dante's love
exempts him from pronouncing judgment.

Brunetto's last words are not of repentance

but of desire for fame among men. He lives in his *Treasure*, the work of his life, and he would have that only, of all he did, to live in the minds of men.

So we part from this sordid group of learned sinners, and Dante fares forward, admonished by Virgil to note well all the words as to his future, which one day will receive their full explanation. The true attitude of man in all the discipline and battle of life is one equally removed from lightmindedness and from despair. Fortune is the true servant of God, and all will one day be clearly understood.

Canto xvi. Almost across the desert, Dante already hears the water of the infernal river falling towards its final bed, but his steps are checked by the cries of some who are quick to know their fellow-townsman by his dress. This was the Roman mantle and hood and the biretta as may be seen in the portrait of Dante in the Bargello fresco, where he and Brunetto Latin stand near to one another.

These three companion spirits are eager fo talk of the beloved Florence. Statesmen an warriors, they are reverenced by Dante, thoug

his inexorable judgment places them here. Two *C. vi.* 79.
are among those named before as worthy of
honour. Of noble parts, Dante worships their
intellect, and honours always their patriotism ; *vv.* 58–60.
but not for that will he gloss over their sin,
though he feels intense pity for their condition.
They, for their part, feel the shame of their
present state, and the chief speaker shows some
desire to throw the blame for it on his savage
wife ; but chiefly, they would fain dwell for a
moment on their honourable achievements, and
learn if the dear city flourishes, and who this
is who comes to visit the sad lower world.

They courteously tell their names, and entreat
for news. It is but a sad tale Dante has to *vv.* 73–75.
tell. There are hardly any now so valorous
as they. Greed of quickly made wealth has
led to commercial corruption, and the fibre of
the citizen is weakened by luxury which breeds
pride and excess. Things are going from bad
to worse. Guido Guerra's impure life had been
a sad descent from the simplicity of the good
Gualdrada, who was a worthy child of Bellin- *Par.*, xv.
112–114.
ion Berti, the frugal unostentatious citizen of
a former day ; now things are worse, and vice

is more rampant, for the love of money is sapping the virtue of all.

One point is noticeable here. The friends and relations of these men were living when Dante wrote, so that his words of doom were, as he knew, making for him new and bitter enemies. Yet, though in spirit he lies at the feet of these men in reverent honour for their true patriotism, he, like Jeremiah, is forced to give his message of condemnation.

vv. 61-63. For himself, he learns by every bitter experience of this gloomy pilgrimage, more earnestly to seek the apples of the Tree of Life, and as he thinks of the darkness he must yet descend into, he comforts his heart by the thought that he will once more see the beauteous stars. This horror is not his life, though he almost seems to feel, when such men are doomed, as if the shadow of horror would never fall from his heart.

v. 106. Dante had a cord girt round him, but now he unlooses it, and it is Virgil who flings it down into the deep abyss that stretches beneath them, and that will lead them into the third and lowest region of Hell. Dante tells that with this cord he had hoped once to tame the gay, spotted panther that he met in the Forest of Error. The cord was worn by the followers of St. Francis, and it is likely that Dante had belonged to his third order. He had found the outward rule helpless against temptation. Now the awful vision he has had has made all fleshly indulgence bitter to him. That experience of the heart which brings a wholesome shame has been his, and he is protected from such sin in the future.

The sign of an outward form of strict piety seems to attract hypocrisy. The region of cunning and fraud lies before Dante, and ere they enter on it Virgil speaks one word of counsel.

Falsehood, in the guise of truth, is coming nearer and nearer as they wait. Dante's will must be firm to rule his lips by the strictest truth. It is well to avoid, if it may be, even *vv.* 124–136. true words that have a doubtful meaning. Truth must be in the inward parts, but also even the barest appearance of evil must be shunned.

When we compare these words with what is narrated later on, it seems that Dante is thinking of his poem, thinking of how he was compelled to tell things, true, severely true, of the state of men's souls as they choose evil, which would seem to many to be but idle tales. He seems to protest that it was indeed the compelling power of an inward divine command that forced such strange, stern words from his lips.

MALEBOLGE

FRAUDULENT ABUSE OF PERSONAL RELATIONS, OF SPIRITUAL OFFICES, AND OF SCIENCE

> Loco è in inferno detto Malebolge,
> Tutto di pietra e di color ferrigno,
> Come la cerchia che d'intorno il volge.
> > *Inferno*, C. xviii. 1–3.

> O Simon mago, o miseri seguaci,
> Che le cose di Dio, che di bontate
> Deono essere spose, e voi rapaci
> Per oro e per argento adulterate.
> > *Inferno*, C. xix. 1–4.

> Qui vive la pietà quando è ben morta.
> Chi è più scellerato che colui
> Che al guidicio divin compassion porta?
> > *Inferno*, C. xx. 28–30.

VIRGIL'S words of warning as to a perfect Canto xvii. transparency of truth and lucidity of utterance form an appropriate prelude to the appearing of the monster, whom, even as he spoke, they watched floating up from the abyss below.

Geryon, the guardian of this region of cunning Fraud, is a purely symbolic creation.

The most hideous untruth is that which clothes itself in a simulated piety. In Geryon we have the appearance of benignant righteousness in a human face, but the strength and the wisdom are brute strength and serpent's cunning. The serpent here, is of course, the type of fraudulent cunning.

God's best gift to man of wisdom, and prudence, and intellectual insight, was that he might attain to the true vision of a son of God. We are now to see the results of its perversion. It has been used to contradict its true purpose. That by which man should have attained to the knowledge of Truth has been used to distort Truth. That which should have enlightened and helped his brethren, has been used by man to blind and overreach his neighbour. The spiritual power has been lowered to the level of animal cunning. This monster is he who pollutes the whole world. Avarice and hypocrisy join hands to undo humanity.

Among the unnaturally vicious, on the edge

of the circle Dante is leaving, are the Usurers; partaking of the cunning of the abyss, they awaken this thought of the union of avarice and cunning. They are tormented by the fiery rain and the burning sand as they crouch, in a stupid misery, bearing their family emblems engraved on purses hung round their necks, instead of on shields, like true knights.

Like the prodigal and avaricious spirits of *vv. 43-78* the fourth circle, they have lost all individuality, and have vacant faces, unrecognisable by Dante. Their souls were in their money-bags on earth, and only their money-bags are left to them now. Having left the simple, natural life of labour, they lost the gift of creative energy, and were tempted to breed money by devices of cunning and deceit. They thought by accumulating wealth to gain a great name, but now that wealth is all useless, and the souls they forgot, and the individuality they buried in gold are unclothed and empty. There was a "glory *Purg.*, viii. 129. of the purse" they might have had, but that would have come through a wise sharing with the brethren.

In the use of the material goods the spiritual

good may be developed, and that we know grows in the using. As we saw before, two results may come from wealth. To it may be given a soul and so it turns into a spiritual power, or it may steal his soul from its possessor and turn him into a featureless slave of Mammon.

Usury represents money breeding money without enriching the world. The direct contrary of usury is the labour which makes two blades grow where there was only one before. In simple tilling of the kindly earth, some have found a purification from the sordid touch of money on the heart, and a growth of the sense of brotherhood with all the sons of toil.

vv. 64-75.   The lowest type here, is perhaps Scrovigni, who to usury joined miserliness. His last counsel to his son was : " In money and money only are power, strength, and safety," and he seems to have wished the actual coins to be kept secure, hidden away in a locked chest.

Gardner's[1] note on this passage is interesting. Dante chooses as instances of this vice, not the hated and despised Jews, but rich and powerful

[1] *Dante Primer.*

Florentines and Paduans. In this he is simply true to his determination to smite like the wind *Par.*, xvii. 133–135. upon the loftiest summits, so that he who heareth may have his soul arrested by the fame of great instances.

There is ambition in Hell it seems, at which "let none admire," for ambition is not a heavenly attitude of the soul. As Homer was sovereign C. iv. 88. poet in Limbo, so here Vitaliano is the sovereign knight of the Usurers.

The true Wisdom can bind cunning to its service, and to such service Virgil binds Geryon. Though white and shivering with fear, Dante feigns a courage he has not, and trusts to the sane wisdom of Virgil to protect him. Virgil, Cf. C. xiii. 28–30, 82–96. who has a spiritual vision sufficient to read his thoughts, answers Dante's fear by an instant response of helpfulness; holding Dante in his arms, and warning the sullen Geryon to descend gently with wide, sweeping flight, he mounts with his disciple on the huge shoulders of the monster, and commences the fresh descent.

This is a long flight, and Dante impresses this on us by telling how Geryon swam slowly, slowly, wheeling and descending, and how he could for some time see nothing clearly, passing through a void, only hearing the roaring of the whirlpool below. After a time he leant out, and was aware of the great evils drawing nigh on diverse sides. Later, Dante gives some measurements of Hell, but they seem hardly meant to be taken literally. The general idea of the form as an inverted cone is clear, and the great dip here indicates the descent into a region much more degraded than that we have left.

We are now to sojourn among the fiendish sins, and to witness the degradation of the highest powers to the lowest uses, involving hatred and deception. God's image in man is defaced, and the image of the serpent is stamped on man.

Geryon impersonates the union of man and serpent, and the tormentors are of fiendish nature, demons, yet with something human about them.

Canto xviii. The new region is described in all its grim
Circle viii. details. This is a place called the Evil Pits, and its walls are of a hard and livid rock. The circle, which is divided into the ten evil pits, is a ledge set between the deep abyss down

which the poets have been borne by Geryon, and another deep descent, described as a well, which leads to the abode of essential evil. Lucifer and a treacherous crew are transfixed there in the icebound lake.

This ledge, on which we now are resting, "shaken from the back of Geryon," is divided *v. 19.* into ten ditches which, like the moats round a castle, are united by a species of bridgework, formed by cliffs which rise above each ditch. By this means the pilgrims can pass from pit to pit.

In the first pit it is soon plain there are two Pit. i. bands of the tormented moving round the circle in opposite directions, and the outer band moves more quickly than the others. There are many spirits, and they move as men do in a crowded street. Dante is reminded of Cf. *V. N.*, xli.; nothing so much as of the crowds on Ponte St. *Par.*, xxxi. 103-108. Angelo in the Jubilee, the first of its race, in 1300.

These unholy processions are scourged by horned demons. Dante had known Bologna in his student days, and speedily recognises a Bolognese spirit passing by. Many from Bologna are here, and well may Dante curse the greed that bred such vices as are punished in this pit.

This is not the sin of the second circle, but the selfish greed that sells others to a life of sin; or, it is the guile that makes marriages that are founded on gain, not love, and binds the victims, perhaps young and ignorant, to a shameful union; or, it is a simulated love that is really only a selfish lust. This is a far baser thing than any mere carnal defilement of love. Here the intellect was clear to seize advantage, there the flesh was strong, clouding the vision of purity and duty. Those sinners ruined their own lives, these planned destruction for others.

vv. 55-57. We gather this from Caccianimico who tries to hide his shameful face, but must tell the tale of his vile deed. It is a true story that he tells of the sale of his beautiful sister Ghisola to the Marquis d'Este, and for that he is in this plight. Of like nature are the other band, who, basely trading on the confidence of others, betrayed and left them. Jason is their leader; Jason who turned his beauty, and courage, and wisdom into instruments of falsehood and selfishness.

Lower than false deeds, come false words. Pit ii. *v.* 103.
Only now have we come to sins of the tongue,
and always now they appear lower than sinful
deeds.

In this pit are the Flatterers who have spoken
exaggerated and false words to ingratiate themselves, words with no heart behind them, making
a fair show of courtesy for ignoble ends and to
ignoble persons.   Such speech is the direct
opposite of the prophetic word, the opposite of
candour, inspired by love, rebuking evil.

This condemnation of flattery is no dispraise
of courtesy, of which Dante speaks so beautifully
in the *Convivio*.   There he speaks of courtesy *Conv.*, iv.
25, 26, 27.
as a fitting virtue for every age.   In youth
it shows itself in gentle words, and in sweet
serviceableness towards others.   It is the special
grace of manhood, shown in honouring others
and giving reverence to all in their degree.   In
later life it shines forth in fair discourse of the
beautiful experiences of life, and in willing
attention to the words of others.

How different had been the flatteries of these
men and women.   Their fair-sounding speeches
to gain some evil end were really unclean words.

Now the speakers are sunk in indescribable filth. By flattery we help our neighbour to sell his soul for naught, and so share the condemnation of those who are guilty of the sins of others in that they hindered them not from sinning. Dante places such sin far below mere sins of the flesh, which, as such, militate chiefly against a man's own true happiness.

Canto xix., Pit iii.

This whole Canto is given to a subject that lay very heavily on Dante's heart. Simon Magus and his crew are here. We have to enter on the consideration of the sins of Public Life, and first we have the materialisation of the Church. To such a pass have the ravages of the lean and hungry wolf brought the world.

All who are in this pit have, after some fashion, bought or sold some spiritual office or spiritual gift of God for material advantage. Of course the typical sinners are Churchmen. This was the canker of the Mediæval Church, that men trafficked in spiritual offices, or, on the other hand, thought they could buy spiritual gifts

Par., xxix. 115–126.

with money. Dante speaks elsewhere of those who were worse than the pigs of St. Anthony, because they sold indulgences to the ignorant instead of preaching God's Gospel of repentance and forgiveness of sins.

Dante seems specially struck by the appropriateness of the punishment in this circle, and the spirit of Pope Nicholas III. seems to see a connection between his earthly and his eternal condition. *vv. 10–12, 69–72.*

Assassins were buried alive or "propagated" in this way, and these men had been the great assassins of the Spiritual Church. They had reversed the true order, and made spiritual things subordinate to material things, and the lowest, basest designs of men the ruling power in Church life. Now the heads that might have worn the aureole of saintship are sunk in the earth, and hideous flames sprout from their feet.

We have to do with three Popes here, and with Dante's judgment upon them. First we have Nicholas III., who was avaricious and worldly, openly practising simony to advance his family, his "whelps." He was perhaps the first nepotist of renown among the Popes. The advancement of his family was his great concern. There were twenty-three years between *vv.* 52-57.

Cf. C. x. 100-103.

C. iii. 59, 60.

his death and that of Boniface in 1303, and Dante takes an ingenious way of indicating that Boniface was coming soon. Nicholas knows the future, and when he sees Dante is represented as being surprised, thinking the writing of fate is belied by the premature arrival of his successor. Boniface procured the abdication of Celestine, whom Dante probably despised for that act. He intrigued with Charles II. of Naples, and interfered in the affairs of Florence in 1301 on a pretext of peacemaking. Out of that intrigue came Dante's exile and all that followed in its train. The end of Boniface's life was tragic; outraged by Philip IV., the Mal di Francia, he was treated with every indignity, and held prisoner at Anagni while his palace was plundered. A month later he died, raving mad. The crime was utterly reprobated by Dante. The Pope was sacred; the man was the more blameworthy that he degraded so holy an Office. He was frightfully avaricious, a nepotist and a simoniac. "Of all the Roman Pontiffs the darkest name for craft, arrogance, ambition, avarice and cruelty"[1] He is mentioned many times in the *Comedy*.   The worst instance of his simony of which we hear was the absolution he granted to Guido di Montefeltro for a deed yet to be done, in exchange for the aid in his worldly plans which that deed would bring to Boniface.   His evil reign is contrasted with the purity of St. Dominic's aims, and he is condemned by St. Peter, who, red with shame, speaks of him as giving joy to Lucifer.

In Dante's eyes Clement V. is worse even than Boniface, and is compared to Jason, the apostate high-priest, who bribed Antiochus Epiphanes to make him high-priest instead of his elder brother.   Clement owed his election to bribery of Philip the Fair, the Mal di Francia.   The shameful conditions of this intrigue were: 1. That Clement should restore Philip to Communion. 2. That he should in like manner restore his followers. 3. That he should give Philip the tithes due by his kingdom for five years for use in his wars. 4. That he should dishonour the memory of Boniface. 5. That he should make two Car-

C. xxvii. 67–105.

Par., xii. 90.

Par., xxvii. 19–27.

_v._ 82.

2 Mac. iv. 7, 8.

----

[1] Milman.

Purg., xx.
91-93.

dinals at the orders of Philip. The sixth condition was kept secret, but was probably to plunder the Knights Templar. His double-dealing with Henry VII. is referred to by

Par., xvii.
82.
Par. xxx.
139-148.

Cacciaguida and by Beatrice, who also refers to his death and to his place in Hell. One more crime was his; he neglected Italy, and removed the Papal See to Avignon, where it remained for seventy years. Dante refers to

Ep. viii.

this in his Epistle to the Italian Cardinals, where he speaks of Rome sitting solitary and a widow.

Great courage was needed to utter such invective as this; the prophet took his life in his hand, and more than his life, for the Papacy was sacred in Dante's eyes. It was the strength of his love for the Church, that lent venom to his words when he thought of the avarice, and lying intrigue, and cowardly selfishness that laid it waste.

vv. 109-111.

The true strength of the true Church is in the seven gifts of the Holy Spirit: Wisdom and Understanding, Counsel and Strength, Knowledge and true Godliness, and the Fear of the Lord are her spiritual dower, and her moral strength lies in obedience to the ten commandments which embody the law of love to God and love to Man.

All these evils of worldliness and greed, leading to simony and fraud, Dante traces to the temporal power of the Church, which he associates with the fatal gift of Constantine to Pope Sylvester. He refers to this again when talking with Justinian, who speaks of this act *Par.*, xx. 55–60. of Constantine as "of good intention that bore evil fruit." Dante believed that the Emperor, whatever his intention, had neither right nor power to give away the Imperial Authority. The man was made for the Office; the Office was not under control of the man. At the same time, Dante recognises that the moral value of a man's life lies in his motives. Why we perform acts is what affects our moral condition. What we do lives on for good or ill in its inevitable consequences for the world.

From passages like these we can arrive at Dante's views on Church and State, or the relations of Temporal and Spiritual power. He believed that a strong Imperial Authority was needed to keep the Church in the right path.

Certainly, when he enters into political intrigues, the Churchman seems actually worse and more crooked than the layman. Hypocrisy is added to self-seeking, because he must persuade himself that he acts for the highest good of the Church of God.

Canto xx.,
Pit iv. We have seen the degradation of human relationships between men and women, and the degradation of spiritual relationships and functions ; now we come to the degradation of science through disobedience, impatience, and irreverence. Here, as in the other pits, we have intelligence playing upon men's lower passions in order to gain material advantage, instead of imparting God's free gift freely ; in all the sin is against the sonship and brotherhood of man.

vv. 10-18. These sinners have their heads turned backwards, and they walk slowly, as men in a procession repeating litanies, because they do not see where they are going. They form an absolute contrast to the souls in Paradise who gaze on God, and in God, as in a mirror, see all things. The saints always sought for knowledge as a divine gift, and now have their life in " Light intellectual full of Love." These sinful ones sought not for the knowledge that is in God; by many inventions they sought to discover forbidden things, and their ignorance is now eternalised, and is symbolised by Dante in this gruesome fashion.

Spenser, in the *Faery Queen*, describes the old, old man Ignorance, who is the foster-father and servant of the giant Pride as walking in this way, with his head turned back, without foresight or knowledge.

Dante's devotion to true science, to the searching out, and the rejoicing in, all the secrets of Nature, makes him stern to condemn the turning it into a minister of gains through deceptions by which a spurious reputation may be bought. The daughter of God is mocked and made vile by such pseudo scientists. The *Par.*, xxix. 82 *sqq.* puerile belittling of science and turning from truth to vain inventions, for idle love of show, is condemned in connection with the study of Theology in the *Paradiso*. The true scientific spirit is one of laborious humility and patience, following out the mind of God in an open and candid spirit.

K

vv. 19-30.　It seems as if Dante's pity here were not so much for the sinners as for the distortion of the human form witnessed by him. Yet Virgil blames him for his tears. Here piety lives when pity is dead. Beatrice, perfectly at one with the will of God, was untouched by the pains of Hell, and poor Dante must learn that pity is not piety here. We weep living tears for and with any suffering that is disciplinary; we can share that and live. This torment is purely retributive; and if we can accept such torment as divinely just, we must rejoice. If a soul can ever be entirely dead it has no claim of brotherhood upon the living. If such death can be, and so the claim on pity die, it may well be in this place, where the sin is that of insolence and pride, searching out things hidden by the wisdom of God, and refusing to accept the human lot of limitation.

vv. 118-123.　Some lines near the end of this canto touch on those who left honest labour to dabble in forbidden arts. It looks as if Dante believed in the powers of wizards and witches who, up to a much later date, made waxen images of their victims, and sticking pins into them day by day, brought about the death of the terrified and credulous.

Now time is pressing, and after a brief review of various sorcerers and pseudo scientists Virgil urges Dante to fare forward. Dante speaks with no one in this pit, and the judgments passed are not sympathetic. Many of these spirits were no doubt men misunderstood in their time, and their magic arts may have been the guesses of a science that was in advance of its day. Our Michael Scott was undoubtedly a man of learning and of some scientific insight, and a student and teacher of the writings of Aristotle.

When we think how, nearly two centuries later, Leonardo da Vinci was suspected of necromancy and atheism, whereas his mind was really full of deep reverence for God's workings in Nature, and his searchings were ruled in every detail by the laws of mathematics, we hesitate to join with Dante here in his estimate of individuals. Not the less, we accept his judgment as to the true spirit of the scientific seeker after truth, as contrasted with the utilitarian, or the selfish, or the showy spirit of the scientist falsely so called.

MALEBOLGE

FRAUDULENT ABUSE OF POLITICAL POWER AND OF RELIGIOUS PROFESSION

> "Omai convien che tu così ti spoltre,"
> Disse il maestro; "chè seggendo in piuma,
> In fama non si vien, nè sotto coltre;
> Senza la qual chi sua vita consuma,
> Cotal vestigio in terra di sè lascia,
> Qual fummo in aer ed in acqua la schiuma;
> E però leva su, vinci l'ambascia
> Con l'animo che vince ogni battaglia,
> Se col suo grave corpo non s'accascia.
> Più lunga scala convien che si saglia;
> Non basta da costoro esser partito;
> Se tu m'intendi, or fa sì che ti vaglia."
>
> *Inferno*, C. xxiv. 46–57.

Canto xxi.　IN the region of Fraud we have already noticed that the sins of public life are generally dealt with.　Simony in the Church is now followed by Barratry in State or Municipal life, and later, the corruption of Commercial life is dealt with.

In this pit we meet those who have trafficked *Pit v.*
in public offices, or used political power for
money or selfish aggrandisement. This is the
sin against the State, the canker of Political
life, as simony is the sin against the Church,
the canker of ecclesiastical life.

The sin of Barratry was hideous in Dante's
eyes. He thought a man was only completely
human when he was fulfilling truly the civic
life. Politics, the healthy life of his country,
is the concern of every properly developed
man. Everything that concerns it concerns
him.

The venal politicians are plunged in boiling *vv. 7-18.*
pitch. That must be the symbol of the clinging corruption of filthy lucre, defiling everything
it touches. The punishment here consists in
life continued in an atmosphere like that which
the spirits made when alive. Now they abide
for ever as they lived, and devils, whose cunning
they emulated, are their dread enemies, more
cunning, less scrupulous than themselves.

The picture is taken from the Arsenal at
Venice. This was a scene of busy activity;
it was the central point from which went forth

the strength of Venice. Rebuilt in part in 1460, after Dante's day, it is still a place full of interest, and there may still be seen the relics of a great past ; when Dante stood and gazed at the labours of that place in 1314 the vital force of Venice lay before his eyes at a time when Venice was still the great mercantile and naval power of Europe. He may have stood there with Marco Polo, the great explorer, as he drank in his true tales of the lands beyond, tales that expanded and enriched the poet's mental horizon.

In this pit, boiling by divine art, is a great lake of such pitch as was used in the Arsenal. At first Dante can see nothing but the seething, bubbling mass, but presently its meaning is revealed, as one of the demon tormentors comes flying along, clutching a Lucchese magistrate, whom he carries on his shoulders. The magistrates of the venal city are, in bitter irony, called the Elders of St^a. Zita, the pure maiden who held her honour more dear than any reward, and who is the patron saint of Lucca, where now all are ready to make Ay of No *vv. 40-42.* for money. Bonturo seems to have been the greatest Barrator of them all, holding nearly all the chief offices, and selling them for what they would fetch.   He was a great manipulator, as we should say, and we are very fortunate if, even now, our municipal life is altogether free of such wire-pullers, who would sell the moral and physical well-being of our towns to suit "low interests" which they serve.

Here follows a horrible pantomime of Hell. These devils are a vulgar crew.   There is absolutely nothing grand in their wickedness, none here appear as angels of light.   Awe-inspiring they are not, though sufficiently terrifying to their victims.   Consider the horned demons *C. xviii. 65, 66.* gibing at Caccianimico, the descriptions in this canto and the next, and the later descriptions of them, as lying in wait for the souls of sinners, *C. xxvii. 113–117.* and contending for them with the Powers of *Purg., v. 103–108.* Light.   You have surely a picture of the proper denizens of Hell, rejoicing in iniquity, without dignity, and without pity or shame.   Truly the most abject of the human spirits has some worth compared with them.   Of the devils *V. E., i. 2.* Dante speaks, in the treatise *De Vulgare Eloquio*, as not needing speech to make known

Conv., iij.
13 5_20

to one another their perfidy. In the *Convivio* he describes them as not gazing on the Lady Philosophy because in them love is spent, and without love the Vision of God, in whom she is loved, is impossible. Thus they are deprived of the beatitude of the intellect, a deprivation very bitter and full of sadness.

v. 63.
C. ix. 22–30.

Virgil has been here before and reassures Dante that he knows the wiles of these evil creatures, and can daunt them now as once before. The obstructiveness here is the same as in the upper circles, but here it is more unbridled, and has a wildly grotesque play of malice and unfaith. All the powers of Hell are arrayed against the progress of one soul towards salvation. Virgil uses the old, ever new weapon. This pilgrimage is willed by

vv. 83, 84.

God for the good of this one human soul.

Dante is very much afraid here; he feels he is surrounded by enemies who will hardly, he thinks, be bound by any promise. Barratry was the crime of which the malice of his enemies had accused him in order to compass their ends and his banishment, and this is vividly present in Dante's mind. He tells us that he feels just as the besieged did at Caprona when they marched out among their foes, dreading treachery. Dante was just twenty-four when he saw that siege, and the memory of those pale faces and timid gestures is still strong and clear. Not one demon can touch Dante, and Gardner[1] bids us notice that not one drop of the pitch sticks to him.

Now the pilgrims accept an escort of these demons to guide them, an escort Dante would have none of if he might be free of it ; and truly, though they must obey and act as guides, the demons will mislead if they may, and do in some particulars deceive Virgil.

We are coming to the place where the great *vv.* 112-115. earthquake of the Crucifixion shook Hell to its depths, and Malacoda gives the date with great exactitude as counting from that time. It is from this passage compared with one or two others in the *Inferno*, the *Paradiso*, and the *Convivio*, that we may try to arrive at the exact date attributed by Dante to his Vision. We need only say here that no method of reading the passages and comparing them with

[1] *Dante Primer.*

the calendar enables scholars to arrive at a satisfactory solution of the problem of days and hours. It really seems that Dante is not binding himself by secular or ecclesiastical calendars. He is thinking of the world's history after an ideal fashion. The Creation and the fulfilment in time of Man's Redemption by the Crucifixion of Christ are thought of as taking place at the perfect moment of the year, the vernal Equinox ; details as to days are comparatively unimportant. The full moon that shone on Gethsemane, the rising sun of Easter Day, fill our minds with thoughts as we read the *Inferno* and the *Purgatorio*, and adjustments of the calendar affect us very little.

vv. 133–139.

We experience a horrible sensation as Dante turns to follow Virgil and the fiendish escort. He turns his eyes and his mind from the fearful guides to study the lake of pitch. He feels fear as in the battle of Campoldino, at which we can hardly doubt he was present shortly before the siege of Caprona. Guido Cavalcanti was there, there Buonconte Montefeltro was killed, and there is a letter, which is probably authentic, in

Purg., v.
85–129.

which Dante writes of the fear he felt that day, and then of the joy of battle.

The most interesting story we touch on here, *Canto xxii. vv.* 67, 81–87. is perhaps that of Frate Gomito, of Gallura, in Sardinia.   He was Deputy to Nino, Judge of Gallura, and, being bribed, he let the enemies of Nino escape.   Nino would not believe Gomito treacherous till he had proof, and then he hanged him.   Nino Visconti was a grandson of Count Ugolino of Pisa, and was much in Florence in 1290, after being treacherously expelled from Pisa.   There he became Dante's friend.   After this he was made judge of Gallura.   He was the "Giudice Nin Gentil" of *Purg.*, viii. 46–55. the *Purgatorio*, lovely in mind and manners, bold and brave; he married Beatrice d'Este, who *Purg.*, viii. 70–84. took as her second husband Azzo Visconti of Milan.   Sardinia, spoken of here as, not Latin but near of kin being subject to Pisa, was notoriously unhealthy, a penal settlement in Roman and mediæval as it is in modern days. It had a bad name for the corruption and cruelty of its "judges," as the governors of the four districts into which it was divided were called..   This was probably why Dante expresses a pleased surprise at finding Nino in the Valley of the Kings. His friend had resisted the temptations of irresponsible authority. He is among the negligent rulers as not without fault in that he left such a man as this Frate Gomito to rule for him.

Michel Zanche, another Sardinian of the neighbouring district of Logodoro, is here along with Frate Gomito. Love of their native land lives on in these two spirits as in the Florentines, and their talk is still of Sardinia. These bad men are still human, and, like Dante, we turn from the foul demons to watch them almost with a sense of relief.

The canto ends with a fiendish contest, first between the demons and Ciampolo of Navarre, who escapes for the moment, though only into the lake of pitch, and then among the demons themselves.

Canto xxiii. In contrast to all the din and confusion of the skirmish, Virgil and Dante move on, silent, single, companionless, like the Franciscans who walk two and two, but one before the other in meditation. Dante's meditations are of danger and of flight, for he still dreads pursuit by the disappointed and infuriated devils. Even as he tells his fear to Virgil they come flying along with extended wings. Virgil, who knows even Dante's unspoken fear, is ready with help, and, careless of self, like a mother rescuing her child at any cost from a burning house, seizes his charge in his arms and, lying down on his back, trusts himself to the slope of the cliff and slides down fast, but safely, into the next pit, where the demons have no power to follow. Their power is limited as their region is fixed, and their unwilling obedience to the law of the great Master is inevitable.

In the higher human wisdom, shown in the gentle personality of Virgil, Dante finds not only intellectual illumination but mother-love. The higher the wisdom the more tender the help. Virgil does not represent mere knowledge; he sometimes falls short in that, and cannot always answer Dante's questions, but he is a true guide and keeps Dante in the attitude of hopefulness; he keeps alive in him a consciousness of the supremacy of righteousness, and can, at the worst, keep him from despair till a better helper

C. ix. 55-60. comes.   In the touching phrase of Canto xv. 54, he guides Dante home by this path.

Pit vi.   The new scene is a great contrast to the last. There all was noise, and hurry, and combat; the vulgarity of the life of chicanery was typified in the grotesque and ugly vulgarity of the turbulent demons.   Here, on the contrary, all is seemly and dignified.   The first view is as of a stately procession of Ecclesiastics clad in beautiful vestments.   Yet, as we watch them creep along, hardly moving with all their efforts, we realise that all is not well with these monks.   Even in the murky light the vestments glitter, their gilding is akin to the ruddy glow it reflects, but the glitter is all on the surface.   The vestments of these " Religious " are of heavy, sullen lead. We are in the College of the Hypocrites.   Like Geryon they had fair faces as of righteous men, but their hearts were evil.   These are the sinners of the Religious World.

Some, no doubt, followed religion for selfish ends, seeking to live on easy terms with the conventional world of their day, but many were self-deceived, their state was veiled even from themselves.   They were used to hide away the

thoughts and intents of their hearts under so
many coverings of specious observances and
external acts of piety, that, even to themselves,
they seemed really to love the religion they
praised so warmly. What they needed was to
tear off their trappings and turn to the Sun of
Righteousness in all simplicity for cleansing :

> "As when the bleacher spreads, to seethe it
>   In the cleansing sun, his wool—
>   Steeps in the flood of noontide whiteness
>   Some defiled, discoloured web."

A religious temperament, or an amiable
natural disposition may go far to turn some
into hypocrites, but fresh air and sunlight are
cures. The keen air of criticism, friendly and
unfriendly, should blow away the mists that
hide from a man what the things are that are
really worthy in his eyes, really loved and striven
after by him, so that he cannot long hide himself in the specious outsides of religion. On
these doomed ones no heaven-born breezes
blow ; they are left with their gorgeous wrap-
pings. It is a fine and terrible touch that they
are not naked and exposed in their worldly
thoughts, but have their fair outward show

weighing them down as they go their weary round, never now to be free from the pretences that once seemed so honourable a covering. Heavy and oppressive, these cloaks hinder all action. There can be no uplifting of the soul now.

After listening a little to some who, with false pretences of patriotism, had wrought desolations, Dante begins to speak ; suddenly he interrupts himself, all his attention is drawn to one figure. All else pales before this sight. The high-priest of Hypocrisy is here, Caiphas, who, in the name of patriotism and with the support of a religious office, condemned the Just One to death, and condemned his race to ages of contumely. He, with Annas and the Sanhedrin, who, along with the Pharisees, represented the religious world of Jerusalem, also condemned themselves. Now the weight of all the world's hypocrisies weighs on them who would not open their hearts to the words of him who testified to the Truth.

This sight fills Virgil with amazement. The Christian Tragedy is a strange sound in his ears. Such a sin had no place in his world. It is strange that there is a note of respect in Virgil's address to the Friar with whom they have been talking as he asks him to tell them their way. His answer exposes the falsehood *vv.* 133-138. of Malacoda, who had promised they would find a second cliff, not destroyed by the earthquake, by which they should cross to the next pit. Virgil's wisdom has been misled by the cunning of the fiend, but he is not for that the less dear to Dante as he once more follows in the prints of his beloved feet.

Well might he love such a guide, and as we Canto xxiv. read the first half of the next canto, we share his loving reverence for the poet, so strong and full of courage himself, yet so tender and full of encouragement for Dante. We are, for the moment, in a new atmosphere; we almost forget our surroundings, and seem already to have reached a land of hopeful effort where all desires after holiness may attain their glad fulfilment.

The opening lines of the canto bring us at *vv.* 1-15. once into touch with a wholesome human life a life of struggle and of fears, as well as hopes, but a life close to nature and with no worse

L

dread than of her stormy weather. The poor peasant in the first mornings of the early spring stands before us at the door of his hut; a return of the wintry weather from which he has just escaped fills him with fears for his flock, and he retreats indoors with lamentation; in a short hour, venturing forth again, he finds the sun has been shining and it is spring once more, in the world and in his heart. So Dante says he feared when Virgil's face was darkened, but before they reach the dangerous pass the sun is shining once more in Virgil's soul and gleaming out in his sweet aspect. The sense of rest in a strong, serene helpfulness that Dante felt when Virgil first met him at the foot of the sunlit hill that he longed to mount, but could not, returns to him here. All his confidence is needed. Ruskin notes, in reading Canto xii., that Dante was a poor climber; the Alps, where he had scrambled, are remembered as the scene of many a slip and breathless struggle. Nature is dear to Dante for herself, and he loves the birds and the lambs and all the life of the fields and hedgerow, but the moral side of life is nearest his heart, never far from his thoughts.

He is the poet of Righteousness.   Here nature
gives to him a picture of the life of the soul;
we have evident symbolism of spiritual struggle.

This is no road for one with the mantle of *vv. 46-78.*
lead. Here, unless there is reality, and simplicity,
and humility, there will be no outlet. Virgil
evidently points to the stair of Purgatory,
the spirit of the whole passage is the spirit of
aspiration. It is not enough to see this dread-
ful place, not enough to leave these sinners with
loathing for their state; Dante's will must be
set on righteousness, he must climb, must be
ready to suffer the fatigue and hardness of
discipline and unremitting effort, never taking
a backward step, but rising "with the swift
wings and with the pinions of a great desire"
for cleansing. The fame so to be won is the
true eternal fame, the real life of the soul, not
that "last infirmity of noble minds" of which
Milton speaks.

Dante has just left the hypocrites behind,
and his conscience is searched by questionings
as to the poverty of his own righteous acts as
compared with the loftiness of his professed
ideal. The prophetic gift is an awful possession

and probes the conscience of the prophet more deeply than that of any of his hearers. It is inevitable that at this moment Dante should think of the religious life as a desperate, well-nigh hopeless climb.

The true religious life, as he pictures it, is all joy; it is a life of song and rhythmic dance, a glad game, but that life is not yet. Some gracious souls in tune with the eternal harmonies seem, even on earth, to breathe an atmosphere of joy and peace, but perhaps, for a complete insight into life and a full sympathy with all the sin and sorrow of souls, some such experience as Dante's of the horror of sin and its power is needed. "Had it not been shortened *I* certainly had been defeated," is often the cry of him who will best help his fellow-climber. But Dante was not defeated, and for those to whom life seems to hold more of struggle than of victory, there need be no despair. There will always be some shining face with sweet guiding smile to help and encourage, some more strenuous soul to urge them on till they are fain to seem more brave and less breathless than they feel. That is not hypocrisy, it is the will answering

to the rally, " Conquer thy panting with the *vv. 52, 53.*
soul that conquers every battle if with its
heavy body it sinks not down."   It is the
" Freewill, which, if it endure the strain in its *Purg.*, xvi 76–78.
first battlings with the heavens, at length gains
the whole victory, if it be well nurtured."

The whole scene rings with a personal note ;
Dante will affect a virtue he has not, and, like
a poor climber, will talk, hoping to hide his
fatigue.   This is not hypocrisy, but after all,
much talking exhausts the strength, and perhaps
there is a touch of reproof in Virgil's words
when Dante would know what is coming into
view after this panting climb : " Other answer
I give thee not than the deed : for a fit request
should be followed with the work in silence."
We are reminded of Newman's lines :—

> " Prune thou thy words, the thoughts control
>   That o'er thee press and throng ;
>   They will condense within thy soul,
>   And change to purpose strong."

The pilgrims do not seem to descend into the Pit vii.
seventh pit but stand above on the cliff and
look down ; it is small wonder that they do not
care to come nearer to the horrible scene.   The

pit where cunning thieves are punished is full of terrible serpents, great and small, but all venomous and hideous. Dante, of course, follows Lucan's description of the Libyan desert, but his mind also reverts to the fiery serpents of the Old Testament story. From these creatures no magic stone can give safety, and there are no holes of the earth to hide in. These cunning thieves are horribly maltreated by the more cunning serpents that cling to them, bind them with living thongs, and even reduce them in a moment to dust, only that they may return to life and fresh agony and hopeless conflict.

v. 90.

Dante says their fate is like that of the Phœnix, yet how unlike they are to that mystic bird that, offering up its life on a pyre of sweet and savoury wood, rose from the ashes to a new and vigorous life, whereas these doleful ones return to a death in life.

vv. 122–151.

Vanni Fucci of Pistoia is associated in Dante's mind with the intrigues and dispeace that arose out of the factions of Blacks and Whites which originated in Pistoia. To the brutality of the robber Vanni joined the cunning of the plotter. No one in the Chronicles has a good word for him, but it seems characteristic of him to feel shame; he wrote while alive, "I have lost the good I might have had through little wit, and not of mine own will." It is the low shame that fears very much the judgment of men, now as when on earth, *vv. 133-135.* and is in no way akin to the shame of a good, that is, a sharply accusing, conscience. That bows before the moral ideal that rebukes and urges to repentance and confession; this only makes the sufferer furious because he is found out. Bitterly incensed against the man who knows his sin and disgrace, Vanni prophesies *vv. 140-151.* evil from spite and to spoil the enjoyment which he supposes Dante must feel in his degradation. In contrast to this the true use which a good conscience will make of rebuke is told by Dante in various passages. The last of these is the seventeenth canto of the *Paradiso*, where his martyr ancestor urges him to utter his stern rebukes, saying, "if grievous at first taste, yet vital nutriment shall it leave thereafter when digested."

Many times have the spirits prophesied hard

things, and every prophecy has taken its colour from the character of the prophet. Ciacco, Farinata, Brunetto Latini, and now Vanni Fucci, all tell the same tale with a difference, and from all we turn for comfort and instruction to the summing up of Dante's life and mission by Cacciaguida in the Heaven of those who fought and died for the Truth.

Par., xvii.

Canto xxv.

Vanni's farewell, or rather imprecation of ill-luck on Dante, sums up his character; wildly savage and brutal, cunning and impious, he blasphemes God and hates his fellow-men. To all his sins he adds a pride as overweening and as ignoble as that of Capaneus; he stands boldly impenitent in his base egoism, and Dante has no pity for such deliberate self-assertion in sin. Where pride is rampant Dante will always have us feel the lowest depth is sounded.

v. 17.

Cacus, whom Dante calls a Centaur, does not range with his brethren, for he combines force and fraud, he is no mere animal-man but a cunning, furious thief who lay in wait to defraud. In these pits we are aware of added sin; brutality is made more hideous by cunning.

In token of this we have at this point a horrible
detailed description of metamorphoses as vivid *vv. 34 sqq.*
as they are shocking. We note that the two
serpents, the one large and overmastering, the
other small, venomous, and penetrating, as well
as the human forms, are persons. We have
travelled far on the downward road. We have
seen the demon tormentors and their claim
upon their fraudulent victims ; then came the
serpents clinging closely to their prey. Now
we sicken as we watch with fascinated gaze the
serpent nature exchanging with the human, and
one sinner with another. Compact of guile and
cunning, these sinners need no tormentors but
themselves, and are at once victims and tor-
turers, for they seem literally turned into the
hateful thing they were proud of. Their joy
was to outwit and defraud others, and now they
are become mere symbols of cunning. We are
face to face with undisguised untruth, and the
dissolution of human society, as we witness these
wretches, mere parasites, feeding on one another,
bent on robbing one another of their very individuality ; souls become brutes, and yet the *v. 136.*
brutes are still souls.

Canto xxvi.

The five spirits who take part in this ghastly metamorphosis are all Florentines, and Dante turns in bitter irony upon the beloved city. Dante's love is sensitive to the faults of the dear home of his youth, to which he still longs vv. 1–12. to return. Here the conflict of feeling is very sharp. The city merits misfortune, and it must come, but Dante loves the doomed city, and will suffer keenly in its punishment. He even seems to wish the scourge to come quickly, for he will need the whole strength of his manhood to bear it. "It will weigh the heavier on me as I grow older."

MALEBOLGE

FRAUDULENT ABUSE OF WISDOM AND OF COMMERCIAL RELATIONSHIPS

Allor mi dolsi, ed ora mi ridoglio,
Quand'io drizzo la mente a ciò ch'io vidi ;
E più lo ingegno affreno ch'io non soglio,
Perchè non corra, che virtù nol guidi ;
Si che se stella buona o miglior cosa
M'ha dato il ben, ch'io stesso nol m'invidi.

Inferno, C. xxvi. 19–24.

Assolver non si può, chi non si pente,
Nè pentere e volere insieme puossi,
Per la contraddizion che nol consente.

Inferno, C. xxvii. 118–120.

TIME presses, and the journey must be [Canto xxvi. 13.] continued; quickly the pilgrims come in sight of the Evil Counsellors.

This is a most interesting stage. Dante's [vv. 19–24.] mind is at the moment full of bitterness and of longing affection as he thinks of Florence, so fitted to be the brightest and happiest city in the land, yet so destroyed by faction and evil ambitions; his many schemes for her regeneration rush into his memory. All are foiled because he is shut out in lonely exile and has no part in the life of the city. Often he has been tempted to join in plots from outside; once, perhaps, he yielded to the temptation, hoping to get a chance to do great and good things in the cause of justice and liberty. The struggle in his soul is told in this canto. It is hard to acquiesce in the punishment of the evil counsellors. Dante pities them, for he knows how good the end they served looked, how good, perhaps, it really was. It is upon himself he turns with stern exhortation against the misuse of genius; he calls at once on his star and on some better thing, the Divine Grace that called him and is sanctifying him, to save him from choosing the low means to gain the great end.

Par., xxiv. 145–147.

The true star which shines with a heavenly light in Dante's soul, and will guide him past the temptation to prostitute genius in the service of revenge, or to use it in guileful ways, is his faith in the Spiritual Reality behind every passing act of life. That faith assures him in his darkest hour that Christ is working in the *Purg.*, vi. 118-123. abyss; that, even when all seems most hopeless, God has not forgotten. So Dante has left the evil fruits of political ambition and its crooked counsels, and is seeking the sweet apples of the tree of Life, the true fame to which his mission consecrates him ; he remains true to his mission of turning some souls to righteousness as he has himself been turned. When we think of the hopelessness of reform that clouded Dante's life, and of the standard of statecraft in his day ; when we think of that other burning patriot Macchiavelli, and how he came to preach a political creed that accepts any means if allied with strength, in order to gain patriotic ends, we realise the loftiness of Dante's soul. Pity that is almost sympathy stirs in him for the spirits in this pit ; but it is Dante after all who metes out the judgment on this sin of crafty policy.

These souls, whose cunning words kindled Pit viii. the fires of faction and hate, or who used under- vv. 31-42. hand means to gain patriotic ends, are wrapped

now in flame ; every flame has stolen and con-
sumed a sinner.

vv. 52-54.   One double flame recalls a tale of strife, for
the hatred of Eteocles and Polynices even in
death, was symbolised by the divided flame on
their pyre.   Wrapped in this double flame are
the souls of Ulysses and Diomed, the most
cunning of the Greeks.   Act after act of cunning did Ulysses perform in behalf of his
country, and by his counsels he brought Achilles
to the war, and gained an entrance for his
countrymen into Troy in the famous wooden
horse.   All went very well on earth, but no end
gained could justify such means in Dante's
view of life.

vv. 94-142.   The end of Ulysses' life seems invented by
Dante as a worthy, tragic end for a hero.
Tiresias, in the *Odyssey*, foretells a death from
the sea, but it is "a gentle death which shall
end thee, foredone with smooth old age."   This
stormy scene in the western sea is, perhaps,
suggested by the Genoese expeditions in quest
of a western hemisphere, the Atlantis dreamed
of in the Middle Ages.   Dante was keenly
interested in all such explorations, yet he speaks

here of Ulysses' venture as the "foolish flight," *Par.*, xxvii. 82, 83. and in the *Paradiso* as "the mad way of Ulysses."

Dante was not a Greek scholar, and seems *Conv.*, i. 7 91–105. to need Virgil to interpret for him here. He who declares translation to be, in poetry at least, an impossible thing, probably read Homer as well as Aristotle only in a translation, and here he hints at his limitation; in Limbo we heard nothing of this when he conversed with the "sovereign poet" on equal terms.

The other spirit who attracts us from every Canto xxvii. circumstance of his story is Guido da Monte-feltro. His voice is heard at first only as the *vv.* 4–15. sound made by a fire, but at last articulate words issue from the flame in which he is hidden, and he claims kindred in speech as he recognises the northern tongue of Virgil. Here there will be mutual understanding, and Dante readily answers Guido's eager question as to the state of his native land of Romagna. In *vv.* 61–66. turn, Guido is persuaded to tell the tale of his undoing. Hidden in his flame, he seems not to perceive Dante's still living body, and so reveals what he would otherwise keep concealed for fear of infamy on earth.

Twice banished and excommunicated, in 1296, when seventy-three years old, Guido joined the Franciscans. At the age when it was fitting to take in the sails and go gently into harbour, he repented and confessed, but the priest Boniface called him out to aid him, with his well-known cunning in strategy, in a so-called Crusade that was really a selfish strife with Cardinals.   Boniface had no regard to his own high office, nor to Guido's vow ; he urged his suit with insistence till Guido yielded, and gave the advice which gained Palestrina for the Pope at the, to him, insignificant cost of Guido's soul.   Guido died the following year, 1298.

This sin appears doubly grievous in one who would fain follow St. Francis, the saint of the simple life who sought to lead men back to Nature, setting their bare feet on Mother Earth, honouring toil as the expression of love to men, turning from the conventions of civilisation to listen to the voice of God in the soul. Dante loved St. Francis, and here he paints a dark contrast to his simplicity. The picture is of

the wily ambition of the priest, a modern
Pharisee, self-satisfied and worldly; of the pre-
tence of a crusade, of the absolute lie of a
forgiveness of one who is not penitent; of the *vv.* 118-120.
worldly fox-heart, unchanged by the outward
habit.   In the *Convivio* Dante tells how Guido
entered the convent, and, almost in the same sentence, declares it is not that that is needful, not
the outward seclusion, but the true consecration
of the heart, the life hidden in Christ with God.

The antithesis to Guido's tale is that of the *Purg.,*
v. 88-107.
fate of his son.   Banned by the Church, in the
very hour of death he sheds "one little tear"
of true repentance and is forgiven.

Like Ulysses, Guido was successful on earth;
his fame was fair for cleverness and valour,
even for piety.   He seems to have been buried
in the habit of a Franciscan, and St. Francis
pleads for his soul; but not Dante's most
beloved saint can ward off the retribution on
sin.   The Will must set itself Godward, the
gaze must be toward the light.

> " For word is wind, but the maistrie
> Is that a man himself defende
> Of thing which is nought to commende."

M

Canto xxviii.
Pit ix.

Quickly we pass on to the ninth pit, where the sin seems near of kin to that we have just left behind. For the first time in the *Inferno* there is a hint of the difficulty of telling all that is being experienced, as though Dante began to be overpowered by the weight of the evil that bears him down. Power of insight, of memory, and of speech, are all feeble when dealing with the good and the beautiful; but, up to this point, evil has seemed a thing that can be measured and told. It is awful indeed, and far-reaching in its consequences, but not of that unsearchable depth which in Heaven reduces almost to a level the insight of the loftiest Seraph and of a humble human intelligence.

vv. 7-21.

As are the horrors to be seen after the bloodiest battle, only more horrible than these, is "the hideous mode" of the ninth pit. In it are the Sowers of Discord. Among them are the Schismatics, lower than the Heretics, as showing the spirit of hate and isolation. This is no question of doctrinal agreement. Saladin and Averroës are not here, but among the great souls in Limbo. Saladin was a great ideal hero of the Middle Ages; Averroës revealed Aristotle to the West; both were builders up according to their vision.   Here we have destroyers, those who divided men one from another.   Mahomet is here regarded by Dante from the mediæval point of view, not as a prophet to his own people, but as an author of schism; he is referred to in Canzone xvii. as the blind Mahomet.   Those Christians who divided the Church are not named, save only Fra Dolcino, *vv. 55-60.* and his story shows us what Dante felt as to the spirit of schism.

Fra Dolcino was one of the sect of the Apostolic Brothers, founded in 1260, who desired to reform the Church from its wealth, arrogance, and corruption.   Dante was certainly in sympathy with such aims.   It is the means that were in fault.   The Frate became leader of a revolt, fighting spiritual battles with carnal weapons, and he held out against the forces of the Church on the hills between Novara and Vercelli till, starved out, he was taken prisoner, torn almost to pieces with hot pincers, and then his still living body thrown on the flames, June, 1307, at Vercelli.   It seems to be as a leader of active revolt that Mahomet addresses him and Dante condemns him.   He was in his aims a mediæval Tolstoyan, but most unlike Tolstoy in his methods, would force his views on all at the point of the sword, and the answer of the Church is in the same strain ; hot pincers and the stake.

When the sword, whether literally or in the language of vituperation or of contempt, cuts asunder the Body of Christ we have the spirit of schism.   When we shut out our brethren from sharing in our holy things, or shut ourselves out from union with them in what feeds most deeply the sources of life, by raising enclosures of dogmatic distrust, we are schismatics. The condition of growth, in the intellectual as in the physical world, seems to be limitation, and where there is limitation there will always be variety, and even in many directions disagreement; but if sameness is a sign of death, the spirit of isolation, the unloving spirit that condemns another, is a deeper death and a more fatal bar to growth in the soul.

When we learn to love and understand one another, to realise our own intellectual limitations and the good motives and lofty aims of opponents; when we gain some feeble insight into the spacious depth of the Universe of Truth, and find our brotherhood in the great ideal of a common service, inspired by love to God and Man, the spirit of schism fades away. Then we find ourselves happy in strange company at times, among those of many names, all helping one another home as Dante so beautifully says, home to that life where love is the fruit of knowledge, and they too who love most know most, that life which is—

> "Light intellectual full of Love,
>   Love of the true good full of Joy,
>   Joy that transcendeth every sweetness."

From the religious world we pass to the secular life, and find those who sowed discord between leaders in political life, and who poisoned family life by evil tales. The sins of the tongue and its instrument, the pen, are spread out to view in their evil results. The two most interesting characters in this pit are Curio, and Bertrand de Born. *v.* 64.

Even here we meet with some fine human traits. In the Pit of the Simonists Dante _{C. xix.} 118–120.

indicates it may be conscience of sin that torments Pope Nicholas; here Pier da Medicina tries to warn two men of Fano to avoid their betrayal by Malatestina of Rimini; all human feeling is not dead.

vv. 86, 94-102.

Curio is named as having, according to Lucan, given Julius Cæsar the advice to cross the Rubicon and avenge himself against Rome, which had unjustly proclaimed him an enemy. The tongue that gave that advice is cleft, speechless even of evil words.

The Empire Cæsar founded was the fulfilment of one of Dante's greatest ideas, and yet that does not lead him to condone the low means. No act founded on Egoism could be good whatever results might flow from it. Dante himself was constantly tempted by the Curios of his day to join in attacks on Florence, and avenge his personal wrongs, but he here stamps all such attempts as evil. It is worth *Ep. vii.* notice that in his Epistle to Henry VII., praying him to come to heal the discords of Italy, Dante uses the very words spoken by Curio to Cæsar, but his motive is not to revenge himself or to destroy Florence, but, as he believed, to heal and save, and bring in the reign of justice and peace.

True to his plan of striking only at the great, *vv.* 112-136. Dante now takes one of the most famous troubadours as showing the degradation of the best to the worst uses. Bertrand de Born is mentioned in the *Convivio* as an example of *Conv.*, iv. 11 [128] munificence, and in the treatise *De Vulgare* *V. E.*, ii. 2. *Eloquio* as the consummate poet of Arms. He however abused the poetic gift and degraded the martial spirit, and is described in old Provençal biographies as setting his whole soul on embroiling father and son. The young king, whose death he laments in one of his best poems, is young Henry, son of our Henry II., who was crowned king in his father's lifetime. The poet prostitutes his genius to embitter the personal relations of these two, just such relations as ought to be most sacred. He also seems by his satires to have stirred up strife between England and France, whenever there was peace or truce between the two countries. It is as setting those nearest of kin against one another that this poet symbolises the fruit of discord in the utter destruction of the body.

He is not merely like the others, lacerated and wounded, but his head is severed from the trunk. To turn love into hate is to destroy life.

From Pier da Medicina onward we have those who sinned with the tongue. Instead of dwelling on the lovely things that turn men's hearts to one another, they have brought to light all that was unlovely. Love, St. Paul says, conceals the evil and rejoices to speak the good. These spirits are at the opposite pole *vv.* 112-117. from such peacemakers. Dante says the terrible picture of discord must appear unreal, but that it is the sad truth if we have eyes to see it. It is only by compulsion he tells things that seem untrue. He is simply stating once more the law of retribution, so that he who runs may *Par.*, xvii. 61-63. read. He himself has read as he walked in the lands of his exile among all the vicious and ill Canto xxix. company into which he was thrown. His eyes are drunken and heavy with unshed tears, and he lingers here more than at the other pits, his heart heavy with thoughts of all the weariness and sin of endless strife and faction, of all the egoism that has wrecked his beloved Florence, and ruined all that could be ruined of his own life.

The time is short, the valley, though narrow, *vv.* 8–12. shows still some space to be traversed, so Virgil urges Dante forward. The actual measurement given here need not be emphasised. There are discrepancies between the various measurements given in different places, but the remark on the Mountain of Purgatory, "as far as here counts *Purg.,* xiii. 22. for a mile," seems to indicate that we are not to take too narrowly the letter in this matter any more than in such others as the date of the poem. The meaning is plain enough in the spirit; time presses, and there is still much to learn.

Dante accepts Virgil's admonition, but ex- *vv.* 13–36. plains how his pity had been specially stirred for one of the spirits. This Geri del Bello is a relative of his own who had been at feud with the Sacchetti family, and his death had not been avenged. He is angry with Dante because he turns away and does not promise to take upon himself, as a near relative, the duty of the vendetta.

The vendetta was considered absolutely bind-ing ; Villani speaks of a boy being saved by Providence from a lion in order that he might grow up to avenge his father ; Dante, however, will not act on this code of his day. He understands the sentiment that prompts such acts, and sympathises with it, yet he rises superior to it, and here, as in the more famous case of \Mosca, condemns the low standard which soils justice with personal resentment. Punishment is due, but it can only be justly meted out when the heart of the judge is purged from anger, and few can be just in their own quarrel.

C. xxviii. 103–111.

While Dante tells of his cousin's anger and its cause, he and Virgil move forward, and are now at the edge of the pit. It is deep and dark, so that only as they go down the bank can they see the sufferers there. It is a disgusting place; the whole man is diseased. All society is sick to the centre; there is no faith or truth. There are three classes of falsifiers here, and except the essential traitor there is no baser crime. First we have falsifiers of things, alchemists and false coiners; then falsifiers in deeds, who impersonate others for evil purposes; and last and worst, falsifiers in the medium of Truth itself—in words—the calumniators. There is surely a kinship with those

Pit x.

v. 37.

who violate nature's laws, but they add cunning
to that abuse, and a kind of thieving. They
were the lepers of society, its moral plague-
spots, contaminating all they touched. The
description is of set purpose revolting, and it
is hard to read it without a physical nausea.

When appealed to by that love of fame *vv.* 109-137.
which perhaps would rather be known as evil
than not known at all, Griffolino of Arezzo,
and Capocchio, who were respectively an
alchemist and a maker of false money, talk
with Dante. Here we have the final degradation of science. The daughter of God is prosti-
tuted to serve the evil element in society. The
sin against commercial morality is not now
mere avarice. Avarice has brought forth its
mature fruit here in utter unfaith. The whole
basis of commercial life is faith between man
and man, trust in the honesty of our fellows.
Trade cannot live a day without that. A mere
loss of this confidence may bring a panic, and
ruin to thousands may follow. Untruth saps
the whole stability of a commercial prosperity.
Florence was a mercantile city, and Dante knew
it was only in righteousness it could be exalted.

The Florentine coinage was the standard for Christendom, and here and in Maestro Adamo we have the typical sinners against faithful dealing, who poison trust at its source. The last line of Canto xxix. indicates the descent from cleverness to cunning. Dante knew Capocchio long ago, and knew how good an ape he was of Nature. Capocchio was burned in Siena, and so becomes Dante's mouthpiece in a diatribe against that city. Siena was always at war with Florence, and defeated her at Monteaperto, when Florence so narrowly escaped being razed to the ground.

Dante girds at the Sienese for their vanity. They are worse than the French. Four of a company of twelve, who formed the Club of Spendthrifts and vied with one another in wasteful luxury, are here, and Lano, another member, driven to desperation by debt and dishonour, we have already seen in the Wood of the Suicides. They had their witty member, who squandered more than money, "the dazzled one" who, for good company and a good dinner, wasted his wit in an idle company. This light-mindedness of the Sienese is referred to again

Cf. C. xxx. 73-75.

Cf. C. x. 91-93.

v. 132.

Purg., xiii. 151.

by Sapia, the Sienese lady whom Dante meets on the Mount of Cleansing.

Dante condemns most severely the vices of the Tuscan cities, perhaps because he knew them best, and all have their history linked with the history and misfortunes of Florence. If Siena and Lucca, Pistoia and Pisa, are sternly dealt with, it is the well-beloved Florence that is attacked with the most concentrated bitterness. Florence, the beautiful city, was founded *Par.,* ix. 127–132. by Satan, from whose envy has come so much weeping; she has by that money, which tempts so many to sin, turned the Shepherd to a Wolf. She is so full of envy that the sack *Inf.,* vi. 49, 50. already overflows. She holds a people avaricious, envious, and proud, and is a very nest of C. xv. 68, 78. malice. She was once full of simplicity and *Par.,* xv. 97–135. thrifty manhood, but now is base and degenerate. She is our perverse country. The *Inf.,* xvi. 9, 73–75. upstart people and the hasty gains have engendered in her pride and excess. She is a C. vi. 61. divided city, and if famous, it is alas, in Hell C. xxvi. 1–6. for all iniquity. In these and many other passages does Dante bewail with sad and bitter words the sin of Florence, which is bringing on her and on him misfortune upon misfortune, hard to bear and weighing always heavier as age approaches and hope is weary.

Canto xxx.

The madness of Athamas is one of those legends of Nemesis so common in Greek story. Rebellion against the will of the gods brings a frenzy, and so works out punishment through the sinner's own acts. Athamas indulged in forbidden love, and then, going mad, he killed one son and caused the despair of the woman he loved, and drove her to suicide along with his other son.

v. 79.

Madness possesses the souls we are now among, alienation of the minds they had abused. These are they who impersonated, for vile purposes, the individualities of others, rabid and bewildered, they have lost their own. Hidden from view in another man's semblance as in a disguise, they had felt the less trammelled by moral responsibility, and revelled in evil. From these Dante turns to Maestro Adamo, the false coiner. He is full of spiteful rage against the Conti Guidi of Romena, who instigated him to his deed, or rather brought him to this torment, and he longs to know they too are in misery. That would be sweeter to his vindictive longing than even a draught of fresh water from Romena's famous fountain to his parched mouth. A vision of moist, green freshness rises in Dante's mind as he remembers Romena, one of the many shelters of his life in exile. On earth Adamo had enough, yet, to have more than enough, he sold his life, and now he lacks the merest necessity of life, a drop of water.

Lowest, basest of all, lie abject the calumniators. All through sins of the tongue are put lower than sins in act. They represent the perversion of pure reason. The gift of speech is the most purely spiritual of gifts to man; it is the medium through which Divine Wisdom should flow in loving words of reasonable discourse from the lips of men. These slanderous tongues, which have falsified words from spite and malice, represent the nadir of this whole circle, where cunning thievish untruth has its lair.

The element of treachery is emphasised by the introduction of Sinon on the lowest edge. He made the Trojans believe that the wooden horse was an offering for the Palladium, and so gained its entry into the city. His treachery was only to enemies, yet he forms a fitting link with the nether Hell, the seat of treachery to friends and brethren.

Sadly ends our stay in this dread region, for it ends with a sense of degradation. Curious, and as though growing accustomed to evil, Dante lingers unduly to hearken to the quarrelling and gibes of Maestro Adamo and Sinon, and well-nigh loses his guide. Sharply reproved by Virgil for his vulgar fault, he turns away, speechless from shame, feeling he shares in the shamefulness of what he has hearkened to. So by shame he is purged from shame, purged by the blush "which sometimes makes a man worthy of pardon."

Purg.,
v. 20, 21.
Cf. *Purg.,*
iii. 7-9.

Virgil is quick to pardon, and promises that he will always be present in his sweet reasonableness to warn and rouse Dante, if Dante will remember. Virgil, the sympathetic friend, now after much intercourse amid sorrow and danger and temptation, grown in intimacy, and of late treated almost as an equal, will always support and cheer the heavenward steps of his friend as long as his heart is set upon righteousness.

THE FROZEN MARSH

Sappi che tosto che l'anima trade,
Come fec'io, il corpo suo l'è tolto
Da un demonio, che poscia il governa
Mentre che il tempo suo tutto sia volto.

Inferno, C. xxxiii. 129–132.

Quando noi fummo fatti tanto avante,
Ch'al mio maestro piacque di mostrarmi
La creatura ch'ebbe il bel sembiante,
Dinanzi mi si tolse, e fe' restarmi,
"Ecco Dite" dicendo, "èd ecco il loco,
Ove convien che di fortezza t'armi."
S'ei fu si bel com' egli è ora brutto
E contra il suo Fattore alzò le ciglia,
Ben dee da lui procedere ogni lutto.

Inferno, xxxiv. 16–21, 34–36.

IN fitting silence, atoning his fault by fresh, ^{Canto xxxi.} obedient effort, Dante plods on through a sort of darkness visible, following his guide and seeking some entrance into the lowest depth of all. At last a thunderous sound, such as was never blown from earthly trumpet, draws

attention to the guardians of the very pit of
Hell. At first, seeing only great masses loom-
ing through the mists, Dante thinks he spies
out the towers of a new infernal city; Virgil,
with a freshly loving grasp of the hand, which
was surely a tender response to Dante's simplicity of repentance, bids him hurry on and
he will see, not towers but giants, standing in
the well which forms the centre and the exit of
the Malebolge.

If the guardians of the circles so far have
been symbolic figures, these are not less so.
Nothing that lacks the human semblance can
fully represent the final human degradation.
Really—and here it seems as though Dante
wishes us to feel this—really it is unfair when
we say bad men are like the brutes. The beasts
fulfil the perfection of their nature; the ferocity
of the tiger and the cunning of the serpent are
gifts of God to preserve the manifold variety
of animal life in the world, but, in Man, the soul
must triumph in love and self-surrender or we
have a monster such as these are.

Power and cunning, barren of love and
working rebellion, the offspring of pride, are

here. We are now come to the full harvest of the seed of pride and envy.

The act of Cain expands, as our view of life and history widens, into treachery against our fatherland, our friends, and the deepest, widest interests of humanity in Church and Empire.

Nimrod, who built the tower that never *vv. 70-74.* could be completed, represents the degradation of the intellect as well as the spirit of rebellion. Stupid and confused, he is alike unintelligible and unintelligent. The confusion of language is here regarded as the symbol of the disintegration of society, and the contradiction of that harmony which Dante held to be the ideal condition. It is attributed to rebellious pride. In the *Par.*, xxvi. 127-138. *Paradiso* the varieties of language are looked at from the scientific point of view, and attributed to the natural changefulness and evanescence of human things. Man, as man, must speak, but how is a matter of natural selection and growth ; the modes of speech are as the leaf upon the branch which goeth and another cometh. These two views of the same phenomenon are not contradictory but rather complementary one of the other.

Fame is longed for here as all through the *Inferno.* We are constantly presented by Dante with the contrast between the high and the base love of fame. The one is a noble desire to live in good work in the day when men shall call our times ancient; the other is a greedy love of renown among our fellows, or a lust for the idle acclamation that dies with the day, "Nought but a breath of wind which now cometh hence and now thence, and changes name because it changes direction." These two are wide as the poles asunder, yet each struggled for the mastery in Dante's soul, and we can trace his consciousness of the struggle all through his writings, till the last, when victory was shadowed forth in the glad vision in which he felt already his desire and will rolled—even as the wheel that moves equally—by the Love that moves the sun and the other stars.

All through this description we see how freely Dante mixes the Sacred Scriptures with the mythological stories. The giants seem to be the counterparts of Satan, here as in the *Purgatorio.* In all alike pride is the root of evil, and discord and irrationality are the

Purg., xii. 25–36.

results. Dante seems almost to accept myth-ology as real history with an allegorical signifi-cance. Capaneus is treated as a real blas-phemer, and Jove as having a rightful claim on obedience. The name of Jove is applied to Christ. We are to think of these old stories as exhibiting men's highest view of God in their day, and its denial and opposition by the powers of evil. Goodness and power are opposed by pride and hate. In like manner, as we have seen, all Roman history is as sacred as that of the Jews in Dante's eyes.

C. xiv. 49–72.
C. xxxi. 43–45, 91, 92.
Purg., vi. 118–120.

Conv., iv. 4, 5.
De Mon., ii., § vi.

At last we reach the lowest depth. It is described as the central point of all the uni-verse of material things; all weights unite here, where the whole material frame of things con-verges and thrusts on the one point. Awful words meet our eye; it had been better for such as we now look upon never to have lived human lives than so to have degraded the God-given nature.

Canto xxxii.
Circle ix.

The medium of punishment, which very specially here is the symbol of the spiritual state, is a lake, but not of fire, frozen more hard than any earthly lake. Numb deadness of body and soul is the ultimate symbol of Hell. God, the spiritual Sun, is Light, and Heat, and Life; this is the farthest point, literally from the sun, symbolically from God. The dead soul, traitor to its own true nature, and to the tenderest and loftiest human trust, is here. The Archangel Lucifer and the human soul of Judas.

vv. 70-75. The faces are dog-like from cold, and Dante feels the ice at his heart; he will all his life long shudder when he thinks of that scene. For a moment he reverts, in thought, to the wholesome scenes of earth; the summer dream of the peasant woman, as she renews in sleep her work on the harvest-field, forms a vivid contrast to the lifeless stagnation of the frozen marsh.

Caina. In the region named from Cain, and so indicating envy as the root of hate and treachery, we find ferocity and treachery united. It is natural that two brothers should be the most typical souls in this part. Their punishment is in a continuance of their sin. Nothing can more torture the soul than impotent hatred, and those two are indissolubly bound together

as no cramp ever bound two pieces of wood.
They will never cease from their furious, impotent, unreasoning hate.

After a short pause among these fractricidal
spirits, Dante descends quickly to the second
of the four divisions of traitors.   Here is a *Antenora.*
wider-reaching, and I think, in Dante's eyes,
a baser crime, the betrayal of the fatherland.

Dante has been warned to walk warily, but *vv.* 19–21.
whether by destiny, or chance, or, as Dante
himself suggests, wilfully, he kicks against the
face of one of these frozen forms.   From what
follows we suspect a touch of brutality in the
act.

The spirit who first claims Dante's attention *vv.* 79–114.
is Bocca degli Abbati, who fought on the side
of the Guelfs at Montaperti, and, at the critical
moment, cut off the hands of their standard-
bearer, and so caused the panic and overthrow
of the party.   Virgil stands aside here while *v.* 82.
Dante speaks with the traitors, and all through
this final stage of the gloomy pilgrimage, Dante
seems to come more directly into touch with
the evil.   It is almost as if here, as in his final
experience in the *Purgatorio* and the *Paradiso,*

Par., xxxiii.
142–145.

there is a direct vision. If so, it seems here to have a debasing effect. If in the Empyrean Dante is for the moment conscious of a moral and spiritual renovation, here he seems touched by a dark shadow of brutality and even of treachery.

vv. 94–96.

The desire for fame is absent here; Dante cannot imagine that a man who betrays his country can have any desire save for oblivion. In the other souls there was still some good, something they might wish men to know; here there is nothing. The stain of brutality is visible on Dante here. Pity has died, and we are shocked; we cannot picture a soul without some germ of good. Dante feels treachery so baleful that the traitor may be hated. To him he may be cruel, to him he may be false. This change in Dante brings to a focus the black side of the *Inferno*. Perfect union with God shuts out pity for the finally impenitent. Beatrice in the opening scene of the *Inferno*, and Cato in the opening scene of the *Purgatorio*, are alike untouched by pity. Dante himsel has been reproved for pity, and yet there is

vv. 97–105.

C. xxxiii.
115–117,
148–150.

something depraved in him when he loses hope, and pain, and pity.

It is a terrible thing to sit upon the throne of judgment. Perhaps it is impossible for a man to mete out justice. There is another view too, that claims our assent. We surely owe to the evil man, if possible, a more absolute truth than to the good man ; he needs it more. To sit on the throne of judgment with Christ, that is, to share His gift of discernment, is, by Christ, given to the humble in heart, and Dante is not humble here. It is when they are purged from the desire to be greatest and grown to the humility that serves that the disciples are to share the throne of judgment. In the Apocalypse also we have a scathing rebuke to the self-satisfied, and it is followed by the promise that when they have been reproved and chastened, and are humbled and penitent, they shall receive this gift of sympathetic discernment.[1] Dante himself tells us the same thing. The Angel who sits upon the threshold of the Gate of Purgatory, the Angel of discern-

Luke xxii. 24–30.

Rev. iii. 14–22.

[1] See *Side Lights from Patmos*, by Rev. G. Matheson, D.D.

ment to divide asunder the thoughts and intents of the heart, is clad in a sad robe, the colour of earth, in token of sympathy with all the sinful souls that come to him. Here Dante dwells on evil only in the spirit of condemnation, and, in doing so, becomes warped to the very crookedness he condemns.

vv. 115–117.   True to his treacherous nature, Bocca degli Abbati deals out to his neighbour that measure he most resented himself. He tells his name; he is Buoso da Duera, who, notoriously avaricious, may have taken money first to hinder Charles of Anjou's entrance into Parma, and then to forward it. The French occupation was a great evil in Dante's opinion, and for that reason Duera's treachery is told. Here, as so often, a Guelf and a Ghibelline are placed side by side, and then we pass from history to myth. The typical traitors of Romance are *vv.* 122, 61.   here, Ganelon and Modred, the one the betrayer of Roland, and belonging to the Charlemagne cycle of romance, the other the betrayer of Arthur in that later story. In these two great romances of the Middle Ages there is a historical element: the heroes are real men, but the stories are wrought into allegories by the romancers of the day. Like all great fiction, they embody the ideals and the moral sentiments of their time. They also satisfy the thirst of that age for narrative of chivalrous combat and deeds of individual prowess. The historical element and the allegory alike attract Dante, and these combats are congenial material for him, who laid heaven and earth under contribution for his great poem.

On the edge of Antenora Dante spies two spirits frozen together in one hole, Ugolino the intriguer, who betrayed his party, and Ruggieri, who horribly betrayed Ugolino, his accomplice. Once more we are linked on to the next depth of evil. Ruggieri seems to belong as much to those who betray friends and comrades as to the traitors against their city.

As Dante gazes on Ugolino he regains his sense of human kinship, and we feel more in sympathy with him as he tells the betrayed traitor that, if he can, he would fain restore somewhat his fair fame among men. Ugolino, however, is [Canto xxxiii.] more concerned to bring his enemy to infamy than to reinstate himself. These two, like the *vv.* 7–9.

two brothers of the Alberti, have their hate, revenge, and treachery ever before them ; it is their woful heritage, and they are linked together by the chains they forged in their earthly *Purg.*, vii. career.   As we look on them we remember the lovely contrasting picture in the Valley of the Kings, where those who had fought most fiercely on earth are comforting one another as they sing sweet songs of submission and praise.   Here we have a very different union, and there is no heat of love to melt away this imprisoning ice.

The story of Ugolino is probably the best-known passage in the *Inferno*.   Its dramatic power and its horror fascinate the most careless reader.   It seems as though it was his treachery to Nino, his grandson and fellow-Guelf, that calls down sentence on him rather than any traitorous designs against Pisa.   However this may be, Dante does not condone his sin, but he claims our human pity for the father's agony and the sons' innocence.   Ugolino plainly loved his sons with a love that made his anguish for their cruel death kill in him the anguish *vv.* 70–75. of hunger ; then to him too came death.

All this lowest Hell seems to be much on Tolomea.
the same level; we have no sense of descent,
yet, as we look on the souls in the third division,
we do feel there is a deeper shade of guilt.
They lie supine and quite enclosed by the ice,
their tears form a frozen horror over their eyes. C. v.
139–142.
We remember how Paolo wept as Francesca told
their piteous story; here there is no meaning or
relief in tears.

Dante is numb, the warm life has all but gone vv. 100–105.
from him, yet he feels a wind blowing against
his face. This surprises him, for it seems to
indicate heat where no vital heat is. This
phenomenon is explained farther on as being
caused by the flapping of Lucifer's wings. C. xxxiv.
46–51.
This wind, which is only explained so late, rose
all through Hell, and we first noticed it in the
circle of the guilty lovers, where it alone caused
the torment of Francesca and the others. Thus
all Hell is linked together by the same unrest.
Every ill flows from the one source which is
symbolised in Lucifer, the supreme manifestation of envy and rebellious pride or egoism.

In this division are those who betrayed friends
and guests, and though we spend but little time

among them, we carry away one of the most vivid impressions of the whole journey. That Dante here betrays his best self and breaks faith with Alberigo we have already noticed. The striking point of the passage is what Alberigo tells us of the privilege of Tolomea. *vv. 124-135.* In this privilege, as explained by him, we see more plainly than perhaps in any other passage the purely moral aspect of Hell as thought out by Dante. He never means us to dwell on the physical picture; that is only a picture by which he tries to bring home to us great spiritual lessons. "You do such and such things," he says to us, "then, as long as you will such things and dwell in such moods, this is what your soul is like." So Alberigo tells us that there are men walking about in our cities whose souls are dead already while they sit with us still at the banqueting-table. A devil inhabits their bodies; their souls are in Hell.

It seems to be more than likely that Branca d'Oria had his soul in Hell before ever he did the deed that showed how hellish was his *vv. 142-147.* thought. Michel Zanche, his father-in-law, whom he treacherously murdered, was not yet arrived where we saw him, seething in the pitch with other cheating politicians, when the mur- derer's soul achieved its ruin in the murderous plan. Truly it is no temporal or local Hell that Dante paints for us when he warns us that Satan is ready to enter into possession of the traitor now, as he entered into Judas of old. *C. xxii.* 88–90.

Alberigo himself was alive in 1300, and it seems as though he too may have shared this awful privilege. He seems not even to know what has become of his own body, but it is when the soul betrays, as he did when he feigned forgiveness that he might the more surely, and as it were in the very symbol of reconciliation, wreak his vengeance on his brother guest, that it is robbed of its body and hurled down to the last post. *vv.* 110, 111.

It is with a grim irony that Virgil quotes now the words of a beautiful hymn of the Passion, as he bids Dante look down on the final ruin. In that hymn the Saviour of Mankind is advancing to the death that is to bring life to his brethren; here the standards are the wings of the Lord of the traitors. Dante Canto xxxiv. Giudecca.

shrinks behind Virgil and seems to find shelter as from a material body. Here are the betrayers of beneficent lords. Completely covered over by the ice, and bending in every attitude of distortion, these men are unrecognisable though dimly visible. Now we only come in contact with three great representative sinners. It is as though Dante wished us here to free ourselves from all judgment upon individuals, and to think of the meaning of the degradation of the Angelic Nature and of Human Nature, as shown in its origin, and in its manifestation at the great moments of the world's history.

Our gaze is arrested first and most intensely by Lucifer, the creature that was once so fair. Elsewhere he is described as created nobler far than other creature, and as the consummation of all creatures. There is a tradition that, gazing on his own beauty, he fell into pride. Now he is " Emperor of the dolorous realm," in contradistinction to " that Emperor who reigns above," and to Christ, " the Emperor who ever reigneth." All the woe of all the world comes through him, through the prostitution of the highest. Beauty, Intellect, Freewill, all have been used only for the life of self, and that means only death. The condition of life is ever to receive from God, and ever to give forth to others. As the faithful angels, in their great ministry, transmitting to the heavenly spheres the divine virtue, fulfil this law, so every creature, from the highest to the humblest, can live only after this manner. The Son of Man, who was the true Son of God, declares to us that He has nothing but what He receives from the Father, and it is thus receiving all that He gives life to His brethren.

In everything we have in Lucifer the antithesis of the Divine. The three heads represent Impotence, Nescience, Hatred, as opposed to the Power, Wisdom, and Love of God. His wings are in number like the wings of the Seraphim, but are useless for flight, only causing the horrible tempest. Smaller meanings, as of race or party, have been given to these appearances, but they are all insufficient to exhaust Dante's thought at such a typical moment.

At the sight of this death in life, Dante *vv. 25-27.* becomes as one who is dead, though still conscious of his death. Again, we see that

O

to Dante to be neither alive nor dead is the most terrible state conceivable; he shares and understands enough of the conditions of his surroundings to realise them in himself. Lucifer is not alone, but holds in each of his terrible mouths one of the arch-traitors of earthly, as he is of universal history. All the treachery possible to man was theirs; Judas from avarice, Brutus from pride, Cassius from envy, all betrayed the best they knew. Judas suffers the greatest punishment; he betrayed the Head and Founder of the Church, the Elder Brother of Man, his own personal friend and teacher, his native country's Hope. Brutus and Cassius betrayed the founder of the Empire, representing all that rules, beautifies, and moralises man's political life. These three traitors represent the destruction of both the Contemplative and the Active Life.

So Man is seen as traitor to his beneficent Master, but also as traitor to himself. Indeed, it is only himself that he can really betray. As Dante and Anselm teach, man cannot injure God, he can only hurt himself. Through the degraded use of freewill he has made himself unable to love and to obey, and only through union with the loving and obedient Christ, can he reinstate himself in his complete life, and regain his true nature.

There is no more to see. "We have seen the whole." *v.* 69.

In Canto i. we had the main thought of the *Comedy*. Our theme was Man subject to temptation, foiled in his efforts against evil, in need of salvation. He must be led, through the experience of the reality and awfulness of sin, to seek in submission and discipline the true freedom which shall make him fit for the *Purg.,* i. 71. Vision of God. In Canto xxxiv. this experience of evil is complete. We have realised the sinfulness of many sins, the lack of self-control, the shutting out the spiritual claim on life, the less than human life to which that leads, the cowardice of the suicide, the vain worship of money, all that prepares man for the fiendish sins. We have seen the fiendish nature asserting itself more and more, till men live only to prey on their fellow-men, defrauding them of material goods, stealing from them their reputation, destroying their mutual love by words set on fire of Hell. Now all is gathered into one as all the rivers of Hell flow down to form the frozen Lake. We think less of acts now, more of the nature of sin in its origin and results. Human Nature is dead, and lies in awful deathly homage to the principles of evil—Pride, Hate, and Envy. Here there is no movement, no word even of blasphemy or rage; there is pure loss of Being.

Dante has passed through this whole range of the experience of evil; its icy touch has been laid on his very soul, but he who has felt the cold of death in his heart is also, and by this very means, to attain to the life of Light and Love. This brings us back again to the opening canto and Dante's great thought of the oneness of the Universe. As Beatrice could descend from the Heaven of joy to very Hell to help her friend, so here, even from the hideous throne of pride, there is an opening that leads up to a land of hopeful suffering, up to the very Paradise of God. Despair can *Par.,* never be Dante's final word: " Church militant *xxv. 52-57.* hath not a child richer in hope." So there be in one soul one thought of penitence we shall

have the counterpart of Branca d'Oria's fate, for
that soul is no longer in Hell; long and dark
may be the ascent, but he will yet come under
the influence of light; he will be chastened and
saved.

Virgil and Dante may not return by the road *vv. 91-93.*
they have just traversed, but Dante remembers they have reached the centre of gravity,
and, as he expresses it, they "took opportunity
of time and place." With much effort Virgil,
dragging Dante with him, arrives, panting and
exhausted, at a cavernous opening in a rock.
This leads into a long tunnel, up which they
climb till, in a new hemisphere, they find that
"here it is morn when it is evening there."

Dante entered the wild wood on Maunday
Thursday, and Virgil and he entered Hell as
night fell on Good Friday; they reach the
throne of Satan at nightfall on Saturday, that
is, at six o'clock, and spend an hour and a half
clambering down Satan's sides and up to the
hole in the rock where it is 7.30 in the morning.
They spend twenty - four hours ascending
through the tunnel to the Isle of Purgatory,
and emerge on its shore on the lovely dawn

of a new day. This may be Easter Monday, or, as some of us love to think, gaining a day instead of losing it, Easter Sunday, when they enter the land where men live unto righteousness.

So we end our pilgrimage with Dante, viewing once more "the beauteous things which Heaven holds." To see the stars is the end of all this toil, to mount to them is the reward after the purgatorial cleansing, and the final bliss of Paradise is to have the desire and will turned by Love, as are the sun and the other stars.